The author's profit̲s̲ ̲f̲r̲o̲m̲ ̲t̲h̲i̲s̲ ̲b̲o̲o̲k̲ ̲w̲i̲l̲l̲ ̲b̲e̲ ̲g̲i̲v̲e̲n̲
to The Rosenberg Fund for Children

The Rosenberg Fund for Children (RFC) is a non-profit, public foundation that makes grants to aid children in the U.S. whose parents are targeted, progressive activists. We also assist youth who themselves have been targeted as a result of their progressive activities. Donations to the RFC are tax-deductible to the full extent of the law.

rfc@rfc.org

This American Family

Growing Up As A Red Diaper Baby

A Memoir

Chris Christie

BookLocker.com, Inc.
2010

This book is dedicated to my parents:
Evelyn Christie,
Mike Shnaper
and
Walter Miller
Their honor and bravery will be an inspiration to all
of us who come after them.

This American Family

Growing Up As A Red Diaper Baby

A Memoir

Sleep sound
Don't awake yet
Your dreams may carry you
Into a world of make believe
too soon.
Robin Christie, age 10 yrs.

Cold War is only cold until it hits you.
Country Joe McDonald

CHICAGO, 1947

On a summer morning when I was about five years old, my mother and I walked into the front door of the apartment building where we lived with my grandparents in Hyde Park on Chicago's South Side. Standing in the lobby beside my mother, idly watching as she reached into our mailbox, I realized suddenly that the letters above the box were not the same letters that spelled our name. "Mama," I burst out, "that's the wrong mailbox. That's not our name."

I felt my mother stiffen. Her eyes scanned the lobby, but we were alone. She turned then and knelt down on the hard, grey floor beside me, taking me by both arms, looking hard into my eyes, speaking in a tight voice. "You must never, ever say that again where anyone can hear you. We could be hurt!" I can still see the strange name, Greenberg, in silver letters across that mailbox, as clearly as if I had seen it only yesterday. I feel myself holding my breath; see the green landlord paint on the walls, the sunlight streaming in the big, glass doors, and everything freezes. Those few moments are like a movie still I carry around inside my head.

...*"We interrupt this program to bring you a special news bulletin from CBS World News,"* stated the tense voice of a radio commentator. *"A press association has just announced that President Roosevelt is dead..."*
   -Columbia Broadcasting System, 5:49 P.M., EST, April 12, 1945

...*At Harmon Station on the Hudson River as the funeral train passed through during the grey early morning, a man said to a stranger standing beside him, "I never voted for him. I should have but I never did. We're going to miss him, miss him terribly..."*
   -Albert Kahn, *High Treason: The Plot Against the People*

The McCarthy era does not date from 1950, when Joseph McCarthy made his first charges. It dates from 1947, from the joint efforts of Truman, Attorney General Tom Clark, and J. Edgar Hoover. They gave the House Un-American Activities Committee its weapons—the lists it could use on witnesses, the loyalty program for which it could demand ever stricter enforcement, the presumption that a citizen is disloyal until proven loyal, the denial of work to any man or woman who would not undergo such a proving process. The List meant that everyone must henceforth watch his or her contacts, where one went, whom one saw—a gregarious misstep into the wrong meeting, a check signed for some charitable cause, a more than casual acquaintance with radicals, could put you on the List and forbid you a job..."
   -Gary Wills, Introduction to *Scoundrel Time* by Lillian Hellman

No less extraordinary than the "evidence on which the government employees were charged with disloyalty was the manner of their interrogation by the loyalty boards. Here, taken from the transcripts of loyalty board hearings are some typical questions addressed to Federal employees by the boards:

Are your friends and associates intelligent, clever?
Have you a book by John Reed?
There is a suspicion that you are in sympathy with the underprivileged. Is this true?
Was your father native born?
How do you feel about the segregation?
Did you or your wife ever invite a Negro into your home?
-Albert Kahn, *High Treason: The Plot Against the People.*

The Smith Act trials which began in November, 1948, indicted eleven people who were accused of being members of the Communist Party and therefore, guilty of belonging to a group advocating or teaching the forcible overthrow of the government. On October 15, 1949, the jury reached the verdict of guilty. They were given five years and a fine of $10,000 with the exception of one who was given three years because of an exemplary war record...
-Howard Zinn, *A People's History of the United States*

Chicago, 1948-1949

Our last year in Chicago, the year I turned seven and the last year of my real childhood, I could still slip across an invisible boundary that separated my family from the rest of the neighborhood and blend in with our neighbors along Greenwood street in Hyde Park. But even here I knew not to mention the strange name on our old mailbox or the scar on my mother's leg.

We lived on the second floor of an ordinary red brick apartment building. Even now, if I close my eyes, every room in that long-lost apartment is bright with memory. I can see the dust from the old carpet drifting in the air, feel the sun streaming in the tall bay windows in the living room, the softly varnished wood of the pocket doors separating the living room from my bedroom. My bunk beds are pushed against the far wall, and the sick dolls in my doll hospital are asleep in the boxes lining the perimeter of the room. Was there a window in the corner? Or did I mix it up with a Mrs. Piggle Wiggle story? Because that's how it was in my family, mixing the real with the make believe until they were so thoroughly blended that it became hard to sort it out.

If I let myself drift down the long hallway with bedrooms on both sides, I come to the end, where the hall opens into the dining room, the center of our family space. There are two easy chairs and a reading lamp where Grandpa sat most evenings, and where I learned to read from the big dictionary I opened and spread across my lap. We ate most of our meals at the dining table in the middle of the room. At the far end, the room opens into the kitchen with a smaller wooden table that served as a kind of counter where Grandma kneaded bread or cut out biscuits, where I could stand and watch her push the dough back and forth, smelling the yeast and listening to stories about people and places that would become more alive to me than the real places yet to come, places I never asked for, places I never wanted.

Inside that apartment, it is always quiet, the street noises blurred by the thick walls. I hear the click of my grandmother's heels on the linoleum, smell oatmeal bread baking in the kitchen and feel safe again, wrapped in the smells and sounds, the air fragrant around me. I fall into a kind of swoon so that even today, 50-some years later, there are times I do not want to rise to cook my lunch or mow the lawn, but would rather lie back, eyes closed and drift into that warm place where childhood was still safe, and life was a kind of perpetual poem.

In the evening when my mother came home from the union office, she'd change out of her good, black suit, the one she wore to work both winter and summer and charge into the kitchen trailing the scent of White Shoulders. My Scots-Irish grandmother would be making supper, the air redolent with warm yeast blended with the odor of meat being boiled tough and dry.

My mother knew all kinds of stories about people suffering and then rising up to convince their bosses or their governments to treat them better. She'd lean up against the sink in her black suit pants and tell about her day working in the union office. My mother's favorite stories took place in her glory days in the 1930's, before she became a mother, when she had been a fulltime union organizer for the newly-formed Congress of Industrial Unions (CIO), battling bosses and sometimes even other labor organizers, the kind who wanted to hog the real organizing and let *her* do the typing. Sometimes, by default, she got the real work, meaning the dangerous stuff. She'd stand there, her eyes bright, holding a dish as if she'd forgotten where it went, and tell these stories about her youth, when she had been young and full of politics. She had helped to organize Chicago's packing plants and its steel empire, giving up her evenings to all night meetings, her days to organizing strikes or union hall parades. Once, she said, they sent a young woman riding a horse, Godiva-like down Michigan Avenue, combing her golden tresses.

"You had to be tough in those days to stay alive," she said, her dark eyes flashing. "One time, someone called the union office looking for an organizer to stop company goons from intimidating workers who were trying to form a union at a pickle plant. Well, the guys were all out, so they sent me. I walked right in the back door of the plant, and someone said they had all those workers in the basement, so down I went. They had them sure enough, up against the wall and were throwing knives over their heads. You can bet they were surprised to see a young woman. But I marched right in and yelled, 'Stop!' at the top of my lungs. And they did." By this time her usually pale cheeks were flushed with righteousness, her eyes dancing. I'd be half-listening, watching for the food my mother had forgotten all about.

My grandmother, standing at the stove mashing the potatoes that went with every supper, would kind of nudge her with one hip saying, "Git out the way," and plop down a pot of potatoes, her face red from the heat. I breathed a sigh of relief and let the potato steam rise into my nostrils and hoped there might be gravy.

On Saturday mornings, my mother wrapped an old scarf around her hair, put on one of Grandpa's raggedy shirts and went down the hall to the living room, where she threw open the blinds, letting the sunlight pour into the tall windows that faced the street. This room stood unused most of the time, except at night when people came for meetings and sat stiffly on our old brown sofa and discussed the "issues of the day," their voices low and serious. Grandma usually hustled me back to the dining room, saying, "Leave them be. They have fish to fry."

When she pretended to do housework, I trailed behind her, plopping down on an overstuffed chair, pulling at the threads of the fabric, and watching her run the vacuum around the faded roses on the carpet. For my mother, dusting and vacuuming weren't real work, but a bane of life to be gotten through quickly and avoided when possible. I always knew that the important work had to do with saving the world. It usually didn't take her long to lose interest in the carpet.

"Never trust the cops," she told me, switching off the vacuum. "They're just over-grown bullies paid to defend rich people." She told me about working with the Unemployment Councils during the Depression, how people like her from the Council would arrive on the scene after someone had been evicted for non-payment of their rent and their furniture had been removed and set out on the street. After security left, they'd help carry the furniture back inside until the landlord showed up and the whole thing began again. Sometimes they could slow things down long enough for the family to find another place to live.

Or the time that, because of a cold, she had missed the union picnic across the street from Republican Steel when the C.I.O. was trying to get union recognition. Chicago police had panicked during a yelling match and opened fire. As men ran to protect their families, several were killed and wounded. She forever berated herself for not being one of them. Her fellow union organizer Herb March had been there and had pushed his young son under a parked car to save him. Then Herb dipped his picket sign in the blood of a fallen worker, took it to the meeting later that night, and yelled, "The blood of the workers runs in the streets of Chicago."

Secretly, I felt sorry for Herb's son, Bob, hiding under the car, alone in the dark, and I was glad she hadn't been there to be beaten or killed, but I knew she'd scoff at these feelings, the way she scoffed at any sign of weakness.

"Being a scab is the worst thing you can be," she said. "Better to be an outright crook than a dirty scab." Scabs were people, she had me understand, who took other people's jobs when they were out on strike. "Never, never cross a picket line," she told me, as if I might be going to cross one at any moment. I'd imagine it then, a line drawn on the pavement: On one side, the sun was shining on the pearly gates of the heaven Grandma used to whisper about when no one else was home--a place where God lived and where all little children went when they died, where her dead baby boys lived now. And on the other side, there were terrible men with long pointy noses like the ones Grandpa drew for me, their faces twisted with hate, shaking their fists at us.

Those scowling faces loomed large in my imagination. I had seen them for myself once when I was younger and had gone with my mother to picket a store. We had been marching around a busy street with signs painted in bright colors saying "Unfair To Workers," and handing out sheets of paper called "flyers" to passers-by. It was a cold day, and I was dressed in my winter coat. My mother pulled my knit hat way down over my face, and it kept getting in the way. I was carrying flyers like everyone else, but was having trouble holding onto the sheets of paper with my mittens. Somehow in all the commotion, I strayed a little out of the line of marchers, and when I pushed my hat back, I found myself standing in front of the store, feeling nervous because I couldn't see my mother any longer. I tried to carry on anyway, smiling like my mother had told me to do and handed a flyer to each of two older men leaning up against the store window. One smiled at me and took the paper, kind of nodding, his eyes gentle, but the other pushed it away and me with it, and glowered at me, his face twisted, his eyes dark with fury. Then suddenly my mother was there, and had scooped me up in her arms, saying, "Never mind, honey, those are the men we're picketing against. They aren't nice people." Then she turned her back on them and carried me back to the safety of the line of our people. But I couldn't help looking back at them, and they were still standing there, the one who had taken the flyer from me was staring off into space, past us. He had dropped the flyer to the ground, and it fluttered in the chill wind. The other man still glared at my mother's back, muttering something under his breath.

Sometimes, when she lost interest in cleaning, my mother left the vacuum cleaner in the middle of the living room floor and pulled me into "the music room," a kind of glassed-in sunroom where our piano sat in solitary elegance, waiting to be played. She only knew two songs, "Deck the Halls," and "The Internationale," and she played them both and sang them with gusto. Even in the summer when the windows were open and she could be heard out in the street, she played them and sang with her usual enthusiasm. "Awake ye prisoners of starvation/ rioc ye wretched of the earth..."

After she finished playing, she put a record on the phonograph, and then even music became a lesson to be learned. While the deep bass voice of Paul Robeson filled the apartment, she told me that Paul Robeson was a great singer, actor and athlete, beloved by many, but persecuted by the government because he was a Negro and because he stood up for justice for everyone. When Robeson came to the part in "Old Man River" where he sings, "We must keep fightin' until we're dyin'," my mother's eyes got teary, and she sang so loud she drowned him out.

Then she grabbed my hand and pulled me into the dance, the kind she called "interpretive." She told me she had wanted to be a great dancer, like Martha Graham, but her heart "wouldn't take the stress." Secretly, I thought she looked silly pretending to be a tree, bending and twisting in the wind. But I tried to match the way her slim body gyrated, the dust cloth held high like a banner, and I let her pull me in. We swayed and leapt awkwardly around the room together, bending and twisting to the music.

On those Chicago afternoons when I was still completely in love with her, I took her face in my hands, touching our noses together, looking deep into those dark eyes, seeing the way the light reflected in them, seeing my own face reflected.

Then we pulled apart and laughed and gave each other butterfly kisses, fluttering our eyelashes against each other's cheeks. I told her over and over that she was the most beautiful woman in the whole world, and she would laugh and say, "Pretty is as pretty does."

But I wasn't fooled by her casual dismissal, because I knew that although my family might spurn compliments as bourgeois, they wholly believed in the power of beauty. She and my grandmother always assessed a woman's looks before going on to analyze her other less important attributes. "She's quite a beauty," grandma might say. "Although a little too thin." "Nonsense," my mother would reply, "You can't be too thin, but I do think her nose is too short. It throws her features out of line."

No part of a person's face was small enough to be missed by their careful scrutiny. It was as if they were about to paint each person they saw, and must first get every plane lined up, each feature perfectly fixed in their collective mind's eye.

According to them, all the women in our family were beautiful, and even though I was included, I never believed them. There was too much talk about my aunts' "skin like peaches." But my skin, they said, "had a tendency to take on yellow," and my eyes had dark shadows under them. When they said I had my father's curls, I heard words like "wiry" and "unmanageable." I would twist those curls around my fingers and wish for hair that was straight, the rich brown color of chocolate cake. But

I believed in the beauty of the others, my mother and her sisters, the tall, statuesque Christie women, perpetually young and apple-cheeked, combing their long, brown hair by the kerosene lantern in the farm kitchen back in Michigan. I heard their laughter, saw them putting egg white on their pale, Scotch-Irish skin to make it even whiter, and watched while they heated the flat iron on the cook stove for the yards of cotton waists that must be wrinkle-free.

While my family yearned for the beauty of the past, I saw only the loveliness of my mother now. When she came in to say goodnight, her cheeks pink and her eyes dancing, her beauty surrounded me like perfume. I reached for her, winding my arms around her neck, her skin silky beneath my fingers, breathing her in, hoping to keep her there beside me. I held her there as long as I could, breathing her in, never wanting her to go, unwilling to take the chance she might slip away like my father had done. I worried that she might go off to a union meeting, running down the front steps, and rush off into the night and never come back. But I couldn't tell her that because she'd call it nonsense. I knew she wanted me to be brave, and I wanted to be a hero, a union organizer. But in truth, on the nights she went out, I often lay in bed, listening to the radiator's hiss, the building's creak, and I turned in my sleep, and I worried.

So I tried to keep her next to me as long as I could. "Twirl, mama," I begged, and she twirled around and around until the green skirt stood out in a perfect circle around her Betty Grable legs, perfect except for the long, shiny scar across the left shinbone where a cop had kicked her with his steel-toed boot.

After my mother put on her serious face and rushed off to the union office, and Grandpa went off to the "dirty factory," I got to stay home with my grandmother and help her hunt down the "filthy microbes." According to her, these microbes could be lurking anywhere, even on the dishes she washed in scalding Clorox water that made her hands slick with suds while the hot, soapy fumes rose into the air, burning my eyes as I watched her rinse each dish in water hot enough to turn her hands lobster pink.

The perpetual war on germs was a kind of daily litany that started with a skin check. For her, skin was a particular harbinger of disease. Every day she scrutinized mine, no change too minute to escape her eagle eye. If my skin looked sallow, she worried I might have caught some dread disease. If it seemed dark, she worried about sun poisoning. And every day I was supposed to report the exact state of my bowel movement. I tried to escape this scrutiny by using the bathroom as little as possible. But this only drove her to distraction since she believed in the sanctity of open bowels.

But even though she tried to get me into the bathroom, she regarded all bathrooms as repositories for hideous, unspeakable germs. "Never, never sit on a strange toilet seat," she warned over and over. "You never know what filthy person sat there last." I would try to imagine this person, a man dressed in a filthy overcoat, his long, sallow hands covered with scabs, his nose crusted with snot. The rare times she allowed me to use a public toilet, she'd mummy the seat with toilet paper, and then wash my hands in scalding tap water.

Sometimes my grandmother's ministrations turned to panic. Once when I had thrown up my breakfast, she bundled me in wool blankets and carried me around the apartment building, knocking on doors and crying. Mrs. MacNamara came out into the hall from her downstairs apartment and put her cool, calloused palm against my forehead. "Fever alright," she said, "must be a case of the flu." But my grandmother remembered her cousin, Mabel, who died in the flu epidemic of 1918 and was not comforted by these words. Helpless tears continued to run down her cheeks as she held me in her arms and prayed to God for help. As the long afternoon dragged on, I lay weak and feverish in the dining room easy chair where she could keep an eye on me, curled up inside the hot blankets, believing I was dying. Finally, my mother came home, sponged off my hot cheeks and sent me to my bed to "sleep it off."

But after she left the bedroom and hurried off toward my grandparent's room, I could hear her yelling. "You're the one who made her sick, always feeding her candy and bowls of peaches and cream to fatten her up."

Then Grandma began to cry even harder and to mourn her "poor baby boys." And my mother went into her bedroom and shut the door, saying, "Oh, mother, not the baby boys *again.*"

But I accepted my grandmother's perpetual mourning, as much a part of her as a facial tick. Those dead baby boys were as much a part of the family as if they had lived to grow up with the rest of them. I pictured them as twin angels, plump-cheeked and blue-eyed like I wished I was, and blond and fat and rosy, smelling like the talcum powder Grandma sprinkled in her shoes.

When I lined my bedroom walls with boxes for sick dolls, it made me feel closer to the lost baby boys, and I started taking in the neighborhood dolls to cure them of things like lumbago and chilblains, names I got from grandpa to diagnose their ills.

One day, I went into my bedroom to get my new doll, Molly, who sat on my bed in a place of honor next to Pooh. Molly was a soft rubber doll with the face of a real baby with rosy cheeks and lovely China-blue eyes. When I noticed she had dirty spots on her cheeks and arms from being fondled by all the little girls in our building, I carried her into the bathroom and plopped her into the sink. I filled it with warm water and rubbed at her dirty spots. I remembered that Grandma used a lot of scouring powder to kill germs in the kitchen. I found the can and sprinkled it liberally over her body. Then I lost interest for a while and left her bobbing in the sink. When I returned to my forgotten baby, there in the sink was a sight to fill a mother's heart with horror. My beautiful Molly's skin had turned from lovely pink to a hideous gray, the color of soot, and had cracked open. She lay there in the sink, gazing up at me with the same sweet smile on her face, while her once rosy cheeks oozed like sores beginning to scab over. Tenderly, I lifted her out of the water, wrapped her in a towel, and took her into the dining room where Grandpa sat reading the newspaper.

I lay Molly on his lap and tapped on the newspaper. He looked at me over the top, his face registering impatience. Grandpa," I said anyway, "I think my doll has leprosy. What's leprosy?"

He lowered the paper and looked down at me over the top of his reading glasses. "It's a disease that attacks the skin, tissues and nerves, causing ulcers, scaly scabs, and eventually deformities to other parts of the body. It's contagious, meaning you can catch it, but it's not usually found in Chicago." He looked down at Molly, resting on his knees. "Is that the nasty thing?"

"Is she going to die?" I asked.

"Probably not." But I had seen his eyes change like a veil had dropped. He returned to his paper.

I picked up Molly, but I was thinking of my grandmother's poor, dead babies. I ran one finger over her scaly cheek. "I think she's got it," I told him.

"Well," he said, "keep her away from your grandmother, or you'll have her thinking the whole family is in danger of hideous infection."

"Don't worry. I'll take care of her," I told him.

I took her into my bedroom, wrapped her securely in her blanket and laid her in a cradle. Then I got out my paper and crayons and made a sign that said: "Don't touch. Lepsy" and taped it to the wall above her bed. No matter how many dolls came to lie in the boxes that lined the perimeter of my bedroom, Molly remained my favorite. The other girls who came to play turned their faces from her in disgust, but I loved her in a special way. I knew she was in need of my protection.

One day when I was in my bedroom tending the sick dolls, Barbara, who lived downstairs, came for her doll, resting comfortably in her bed in the hospital. I wouldn't give it to her, so she went downstairs. Soon she was back with her mother in tow. I could hear their voices out in the hall. They must have explained the situation because my grandmother came clicking down the hall and opened my bedroom door. "Christine, do you have this little girl's doll?"

My throat burned with indignation. "She's sick," I said.

"Well," said Grandma, her eyes smiling at me, "Barbara wants to take her home now."

"She can't leave," I said.

"Now, young lady..."she began.

But in a moment of inspiration I knew what to say. "It's like back on the farm when your baby boys got sick with whooping cough, and you always say you should have called the doctor sooner!"

I heard her indrawn breath, her eyes stopped smiling, and for a moment I thought she might be mad, but her voice was gentle. "I'm very sorry," she said, "but the doll belongs to Barbara Jean, and you'll have to give it back." Then she went out in the hall, and I heard her tell them that I'd be out in a minute. I stood there, not sure what to do, but there didn't seem to be any choice, so after a bit, I took the doll out and handed her to Barbara. I thought she'd be mad, but she actually looked scared. Her mother looked mad, though.

After they left, I slouched into the kitchen. Grandma was at the sink washing dishes. I went up and stood beside her, watching her soap the glasses, her knuckles red and slick with bubbles. The air smelled faintly of Clorox. I stood there feeling sad and spent, vaguely uneasy because she was unusually quiet. "Life is real and life is earnest," she said finally.

"Her doll really was sick," I said.

She looked down at me then, her eyes sad like they got on those days nobody talked about except in whispers, when she took to her bed with the "lumposy." On those days, she lay in her dark bedroom with the covers pulled up around her, and tears slid down her cheeks as she remembered her two lost baby boys, the ones she failed to protect against the germs.

We lived with my grandmother's sadness, a kind of invisible disease, one that manifested in sudden attacks that must be tolerated if not fully understood. I think I always knew that when grandma cried for those dead babies, she cried for all of us, for my mother who never cried over my father, for my grandfather's unshed tears over his lost farm, as if she had tapped into the vein of sadness that ran deep underneath our family life.

On this afternoon, she stood at the sink rinsing the glasses, and I leaned my head up against her apron, smelling the familiar mixture of Clorox and starch. "I know, precious," she sighed, "it's hard to be happy sometimes in this old world, dontcha know?" She reached down, lifting a curl gently, delicately, with the tip of one wet finger.

Later, after the dishes were washed and rinsed in water laced with Clorox, then stacked in the dish rack to be sanitized by the air, she hung up the dish rag to dry, took off her apron and laid it carefully over the back of a kitchen chair, gathered up her crochet bag, and we went into the dining room. She sat with her back straight against a chair, her brown suede pumps barely touching the floor, and the bright yarn spilled across her lap. I stood in back of her and unpinned her ropes of hair. My grandmother's once glossy brown hair had turned iron grey, and she anchored it to her head with dozens of hairpins. "Let's pretend," I said, "that you are a rich lady who's come in for a do." I could never play this kind of game with my mother-- too frivolous, and besides, I knew she didn't like rich people.

Grandma, on the other hand, showed a rebellious streak toward her husband and daughter, who were aligned in their hatred of money. She often praised material goods to me in loud stage whispers, doting especially on satin and hand-made lace. Or, even more daring, she told me Bible stories or recited little verses to me about God. She knew that my mother and grandfather were allied against her in their belief that all organized religion was an "opiate for the masses." But grandma had a soft spot for God. "Don't ever forget that He loves little children," she told me. This was supposed to comfort me, but it only made me curious. I was afraid, though, to press her for details because God could easily become a direct route to the "poor dead baby boys." I pictured them cotton-wrapped, blond haired angels, dead for some forty years, but still lingering inside our family's collective memory.

Usually, the "let's pretend" games became a secret button that, once pushed, allowed grandma to reach back into the days of her youth, when she had been the thin, pale daughter of a family that was well-off by small town standards of her day. While I combed and smoothed the thick hair until it shone, I waited for her to take out the past and shake it out like the folds of a summer dress, shake it until the summer nights in Michigan surrounded us and crowded Chicago from the room.

"My mother, Elizabeth Miles," she told me, "had the most beautiful hair in town. When I was a girl, I loved to watch her brush it at night. When she got dressed up and went to town, folks said she looked like she had just stepped out of a bandbox." Not knowing what a bandbox was, I pictured my great-grandmother rising out of a cardboard box like a large Christmas doll. "I couldn't hold a candle to her," grandma said, "though I tried. Used to even wash my soft shoes and hang them on the line to dry at night. I kept my skin pale by eating nothing all day but tealeaves. I used to faint at the drop of a hat." And she laughed in amazement at her own foolishness, but at the same time, I heard pride in the laughter, and it worried me. I bit my lip and thought about my own olive skin.

She loved talking about her "beaux," about the one who took her out in his rowboat and tried to kiss her. Indignation crackled in her voice. "But I fixed him. I made him get out of the boat and swim back to shore. Soon after, he caught pneumonia and died. Wasn't that awful?" But when she turned her head toward me, I could see her eyes danced with delight.

"You let grandpa kiss you," I reminded her. Secretly, I felt a little sorry for that boyfriend.

She gave a laugh then. "Your grandfather was the handsomest man on the dance floor, so tall and graceful. His sister Edith introduced us at a dance at Lake Placid. Everyone went there in the summers. Used to go with my cousins Marjorie and Mable; we were like sisters." She stopped and sighed, like she did whenever she hit a rough spot, and there were a lot of these sad places where her voice might trail off. "Poor, darling Mabel," she continued after a moment, "When she died, I lost my best friend in the whole world."

"What about grandpa?" I asked, wanting to get her off the sad stuff and back on the story of courtship.

She gave a little sniff. "You know," she said, "I was considered a 'catch.' We were the first family in the town of Leslie, Michigan to have an indoor bathroom." She said this with pride while I wondered why, if she felt so proud of this bathroom, she hated them so much now. "Besides," she said, "boys like girls who are fun and lively, dontcha know?" She looked up at me as if to impress it on me. I wasn't sure exactly what it meant to be "lively," but I was pretty sure I wasn't. I knew it had something to do with the way my grandmother's eyes laughed up at the druggist on the corner, the way she kind of sparkled when a man was nearby. "When I met your grandfather, I was already engaged to marry a wealthy candy merchant. He wanted to put my picture on billboards. 'Course my father said no to that. Wouldn't hear of such a thing. But then your grandfather came along, tall and handsome and swept me off my feet, and he was the first man I let kiss me on the lips," she said, giggling delightedly. "And before you could say Jack Robinson, that old candy merchant was gone from my mind.

One day when your grandfather came calling, I said to my mother, 'By the way, I'm off to marry Clare today.' Then I jumped into the buggy, and with a flick of the whip, we were off to a justice of the peace." She laughed with fresh delight. "Well, that was that, and they had to live with it. Mother always liked Clare anyway. But my dad was furious. He wanted me to marry money, and of course, the Christies were poor as church mice. Clare never forgave my dad for looking down his nose at Clare's family."

She always stopped telling the story of her marriage right after the elopement. Then she sighed and said, "Well, all my descendents can carry a tune," as if that summed it all up. I was still trying to make curls, looping and pinning her hair in place, and we sat in silence a moment before she looked down at her hands twisting a Kleenix in her lap, sighed and said, "Oh dear."

I peered around her head, trying to get a glimpse of her face to see if she were crying. I knew the dark eyes would be duller now, her mouth pursed. "You look beautiful," I lied. Everywhere I had tried to make curls, her hair stood up in tufts around her head.

"Time to put the kettle on," she said. The tea kettle would be left to boil dry on the stove, a kind of lament, a tonic, a song. Her eyes cleared, the twinkle came back when she looked up at me, and she went off to the kitchen humming to herself, her tiny feet making clicking sounds on the linoleum as she walked briskly, delicately, almost dancing out to the kitchen, the strains of a long ago waltz floating through the air.

Later, when my mother came home, Grandma came to meet her with her coat on and her cheeks rouged into red spots, but she hadn't touched her hair. "Tea's on," she said.

My mother looked at her with a mixture of awe and irritation. "Surely, mother, you're not going out like that!"

My grandmother lifted her chin and some pins jiggled loose and fell to the rug. "I certainly am. Anyone who doesn't like it doesn't have to look at me." She strode briskly through the door.

I went into the living room and knelt in the big, easy chair in front of the window. I watched as my grandmother sailed down the street, head held high as if she were wearing a crown, trailing pins as she went. I saw her pause to wave and call to Mrs. MacNamara, who turned her head and stared after my grandmother as she made her way down the block. One long coil of hair had come undone and fanned out behind her like a tail as she walked.

On winter evenings after supper, Grandpa sat in his easy chair in the dining room with the newspaper spread out across the lap of the overalls he still wore, even though the farm was long gone, lost to the "God damned banks," was how he put it. Unlike my mother and grandmother, who talked all the time, he mostly kept quiet. But sometimes, he'd suddenly notice me wandering through the apartment, and if he was in the mood for talking, he'd push aside his newspaper. He, too, liked to instruct me in the ways of the world.

Unlike my grandmother, he didn't go in for telling romantic stories about the past. I heard him tell my grandmother that she was going to "fill the child's head with pretty stories when she ought to live in the real world." And he leaned down and punctuated his sentence by sending a long stream of tobacco juice into the tin can at his feet. As a kind of correction, he'd teach me how to spell words, like the day he taught me to spell the word *imperialist,* spelling it over and over until he was sure I had it. He'd catch me as I walked past his chair on my way into the kitchen. "Christine," he'd call out in a loud tone, "What is Great Britain, Christine?"

"Great Britain is an imperialist country," I'd say.

"Spell 'imperialist.'" After I spelled it correctly, he looked pleased, shaking his head and saying in mock disbelief to the room at large, "Even the *child* knows that Great Britain is an imperialist country."

But if he was in the right mood, he'd put the paper down, get out a pencil and draw Baddy Boys for me, making them into the cowboys I was so crazy for, putting hats on their pointy heads, spurs on their stick legs and boots on their skinny feet. "The thing about cowboys," he said, pronouncing it *cooboys*, "is that out on the prairie all day, they never got the chance to wash their underwear, so they stank to high heaven." Then he sang, tapping his boot in rhythm. "Rye tune like-a-day, rye tune-like-a-day/ rye tune like a tune, like a da-de-ay." Then he drew a horse so skinny his backbone made a ridge when he bent his head to throw off the Baddy Boy sitting on its back waving his cowboy hat, and under it he wrote: Christine's Future Husband.

Sometimes grandpa drew the factory where he went every morning to work, a filthy place according to my grandmother, "Not like good, clean farm dirt atall." Grandpa drew a tall building with smoke billowing from its chimneys, closed on the sides with tiny, high windows, but he left the front wall open to view. Inside the building, he drew a huge furnace and a dozen little men with stick legs toting buckets and carrying large bundles, some of them bent over under the weight. Then he drew a large stick man with a long, reptilian nose opening on a mouth filled with scraggly teeth and labeled him "The Boss." When he was finished, he leaned back and chuckled.

One day I had been sitting in Grandpa's chair dreaming and eating a Baby Ruth candy bar. Grandma snuck them to me, putting a finger across her lips, which meant: don't tell your mother. We both knew she didn't approve of sweets for children. I was letting the chocolate melt in my mouth, the sugar coating the back of my throat, when the doorbell rang.

When I opened the front door, I saw it was Grandpa coming slowly up the stairs, not walking like himself at all, but holding onto a banister, his head bent. When he came around the bend, he saw me standing there. He dropped his hand, his back straightened, and he smiled at me. Even in the dim hall, I saw his face had lost all its color. Then he did a thing I had never seen him do in the daytime. Still smiling, nodding hello, he walked past me down the hall and went into his bedroom. I stood in the doorway, vaguely nervous at this odd behavior, and watched him bend over ever so slowly and pull off his boots, letting them hit the floor with a clunk. Then he lay down on top of the covers, still wearing his work clothes, and he stayed there all afternoon, perfectly still in the dim light, his hands laced across his chest. Later, I heard he had fallen at work on a piece of metal that pierced him to the bone.

The next day he was back in his easy chair reading the newspaper. When I came by, he put down the paper and drew the fiery inferno inside his factory. He pointed to the little stick men shoveling coal into a giant furnace, and he said, "Working people got to stick together." I knew I wanted to be on his side.

He leaned forward in his chair and spread his hands out in front of him, regarding them as if they were fine, old tools that had served him well. "These hands have milked a thousand cows and pulled calves from their mother's bellies," he told me. As he talked, I could see his father's fields stretching out as far as the eye could see, could feel the sweat running down his back as he and his brother Joe loaded the hay wagon and cleared the rocky soil by hand. His huge fists opened and closed on the arms of his chair. "I became a man at the age of nine when my dad fell off a hay wagon." His voice always grew cautious when he talked about his father, who had gradually sold off the family land for cash whenever they hit a bad time. He shook his head in amazement over the idea of selling land, the most precious possession a man could own, the thing he had lost forever.

Sometimes I could nudge him into talking about his family life, about his seven brothers and sisters, and how they stood around the piano at night with his mother, my great grandmother, Helen Robinson, and sang songs

When he talked about his mother, her name rolled off his lips. "There never lived a more proper woman. Gave us our lessons every night in front of the fireplace after chores were done. Never swore but once in her life. One day she ran into the kitchen to get a burning pie out of the oven and dropped a tray of needles and pins. 'Damn it anyway,' she said." Then he stopped and grinned and rubbed a hand over his bald head, tickled by his memories of her.

"What kind of pie?" I wanted to hear their names--apple, peach, cherry--as if the sound gave both sustenance and substance, and I could start to feel the sugar in the back of my throat. But like my mother, he wasn't interested in talk about food. He wanted to tell about all the hard work he and his brother had done, all the rocks they had carried, all the hay pitched and baled.

He took me back to that last farm, the one with the apple orchard and a hayloft to jump in. Even, my mother told me, a real play house for my mother and her sisters. Grandpa talked about how he learned about "class struggle" from an organizer who belonged to a local political group called the "Proletarian Party" and came to the town of Leslie to give a speech. Grandpa invited them back to the farm, and grandma fed them pie. That winter, he and my mother and my uncle spent their evenings in front of the fire reading *Das Kapital,* passing the pages back and forth between them.

"Look what happened to me, Dolly," he told me. "I worked my guts out my whole life, and then lost it all in '36." And his face grew still as he remembered the obstacle he couldn't budge, the thing that had beat him and changed his world forever.

"While we ate potatoes and milk gravy," he said, "Mrs. Hoover drove away from the White House with a truckload of fancy ball gowns. While working people were lining up in bread lines and jumping out of windows, the rich just got richer."

I wasn't sure if I was more fascinated by the thought of starving people or the thought of all those pretty dresses. But of course I didn't tell him that, because I knew he already thought I had too many toys, and I didn't want him to think I was like Mrs. Hoover. Instead, I sat silent, holding my breath, waiting for him to go on pulling me into his life. "Some banker," he said, his lip curling in disgust, "some fellow whose white hands had never seen an honest day's work, pushed some paper across a desk, slick as a whistle. Oh, it was legal alright, Dolly, but they stole my land, and don't you ever forget it!"

And I would remember his voice, husky with feeling, as he leaned toward me in his urgency to make me understand. "Not much worth fighting over in this old world, Dolly. But land and justice, they're worth dying for." Then he reached down and wrapped his thick fingers around my skinny ones, gently making them disappear inside his hands, the veins thick and blue, a landscape of wrinkles. Entwined, my hands caught in his, the light from his reading lamp spilling over us, we waited together in the darkening room. I, held captive by his grief, holding my breath waiting for him to look up, and when he finally did, I saw the tears, unshed and glistening, frozen in his eyes the color of ice.

Whenever my other grandmother, Grandma Sarah, came to visit, she brought me lace hankies wrapped in cellophane. Grandma met her at the door, wiping the flour off her hands on the cotton apron she wore to cover her good housedresses. Then she ushered Grandma Sarah into our apartment and went muttering back to the kitchen. I always took her into our living room, the room reserved for company. She would settle her stocky body on the overstuffed sofa, take off her babushka, shrug out of her black coat, pat her dark hair nervously, and begin to cry.

Sometimes just looking at me seemed to make her cry. "Poor little orphan," she'd say, her large eyes filling with tears. Almost immediately, I began to distance myself, not wholly attending to her. I would let my eyes drift through the dimness, skim the closed venetian blinds, roam the armchairs and tables posted along the walls like sentries. Soon Grandma Sarah would begin her litany. "My poor, dead son, oh, I have lost my son," and she would cry noisily, wiping at her eyes with a linen handkerchief.

Eventually, she stopped crying and talked to me, but I never remembered what we talked about, as if her tears washed the words from my memory. Starved as I was for any bits I could glean about my father, our conversations remained a complete blank. Sometimes she spoke to me in English, other times in Yiddish. What I mostly remembered about her was the terrible urgency in her eyes as she searched my face and cried.

On our last visit, just before we left Chicago, she leaned toward me and took my hand, "Promise you'll write to me," she said. "I will get someone to read your letters to me."

"Can't you read them yourself?" I was shocked at the thought of a grown-up who couldn't read, given the passionate reading habits in our household.

"Not English," she said. I was still confused. "What do you read then?"

Now, she looked surprised. "Why, Hebrew, of course," she said. "You know a little Yiddish, maybe?"

"No, I don't know any," I told her. In truth, I had only a vague idea about what it meant to be Jewish. Sometimes grandma would say my father had been "Jewish, but he was a blond." She'd say it in a kind of whisper and then talk about how handsome he had been. I knew I got my green eyes from him and my dark hair from my mother, although my curls came from my father. My mother's hair felt soft to the touch and smooth. She struggled to get a brush through mine. But it had never occurred to me that being Jewish might have anything to do with language or that Grandma Sarah might speak anything other than English.

"It doesn't matter," she said in a sad voice. And she began to recite a verse from her childhood, a beautiful verse she said I must remember, so that I could tell it to my children, and then they would understand something about this family back in Russia that I would never know. I don't remember a word of that verse, but this is what I do remember: "You will be a beauty, Christine," she said, a rare smile flitting across her face. "Georgia, Russia is known for the most beautiful women in the world."

Every time my mother said my hair was wiry and unmanageable or someone in school laughed at my curls, I'd remember what Grandma Sarah said to me, and those words lessened the sting of it a little.

Whenever I remembered Grandma Sarah, I saw her as she was on her last visit, sitting on the overstuffed sofa, black babushka in her lap, her eyes soft with the love of me as she handed me the packet of handkerchiefs and patted my curls, blessing something unlovable about me, something wiry and dark. But I never wrote to her, not even once during all those years.

After she put on her babushka and left, my other grandmother took the cellophane package and put it away in a dresser drawer with all the other unopened packages. "Imagine," she snorted with disgust, "giving a child something so unsanitary." She shook her head in dismay. "Better wash your hands," she added, waggling her finger at me. Then she went off to the kitchen, her gray suede pumps clicking on the linoleum.

I didn't understand just how these pristine packages came to be filled with the dangerous bacteria my mother and grandmother constantly guarded us against. Sometimes when no one was around, I'd go into my grandparents' bedroom, open the drawer and touch the dozen little packages lying innocently among grandma's underwear. They made a crackling noise when I fingered the tiny embroidered flowers and scalloped edges of lace, but as much as I stared at them, they never revealed this mystery locked securely away within their folds.

After Grandma Sarah's last visit, I went off to find my mother, who was curled up on her bed reading the paper. When she saw me standing by the bed, she looked over the paper and smiled, "Did you have a good visit?"

"Why doesn't anyone like Grandma Sarah?" I asked.

My mother sighed and turned back to the paper. "She never appreciated your father when he was alive, so what good are her tears now?"

If she didn't appreciate him, why then did she cry all the time over him, I wondered. But I could tell my mother didn't really want to talk about it.

I would put Grandma Sarah's face out of my mind, try to forget the moist eyes that seemed to plead with me for something I couldn't give her.

Maybe she wanted me to join her in sadness, but I couldn't. Other people cried over my father, but I never did. I always felt as if his death was something apart from me, something not really my business.

Sometimes I pressed my family for a few more facts about my father, like what, exactly, did this father of mine do before he disappeared?

"*Do?*" they would ask, vaguely. "Why he loved you. You were the first person he wanted to see when he came home on leave, and he always brought you presents enough for a princess."

Where were the presents, I wondered? But I never asked. I figured they must be put away like Grandma Sarah's handkerchiefs. When my other grandmother said, "He went off to kill Hitler and didn't come back," it didn't help me understand what had happened to him. She made it sound like he might still be out there somewhere, combing the German countryside.

One night when I was still quite small, and my mother was tucking me into bed, wearing her green circle skirt, which meant going someplace special, she bent to kiss me, and I felt the soft skin brush my cheek, but also the familiar fear that started in my stomach whenever she left me to go out at night. I took a deep breath, taking in the sweet gardenia smell of her, and asked, "Is daddy dead?"

She stopped smoothing the sheets, startled, fear in her eyes and said, "Yes." That was it, the only time I ever remember talking to her about his death. But it was like everything else my mother had forgotten. She could remember the color of a dress she wore to a union picnic, but not the day my father died.

Instead of real information, I had a set of father facts to pull out and rifle through like baseball cards. I knew he liked lox and bagels for breakfast, that he broke a world's running record, and that he had his room in college insulated so he could study in perfect silence. I liked this image of my father as a serious young man, bent over his books. I knew he and my mother met at a dance for "progressives" and that they were not speaking the day they got married on their lunch hour by a justice of the peace, bringing their dentist as a witness. I also knew that he was handsome, she had loved him, and most important, he had "good politics."

Usually if I asked anyone in my family for information they didn't want to give me, they'd say, "Politics," or else they'd say something so totally off the subject that I got distracted and forgot to dig for the real answer. One time I asked where they had lived when I was a baby, before Greenwood Street, and my mother looked pensive, then said, "We always went to Mike's brother's house for dinner, but then he and your father would start screaming at each other over the roast beef. On the way home, I'd say I wasn't going any more, but Mike always said, 'Well, the food's good.'" Then she narrowed her eyes at me and said, "Food is just fuel."

I had only one picture of my father, a picture I found in an old pile of family photos a long time ago. On the back, written in my mother's handwriting, it says, "Spring, 1944," It is a picture of a man wearing an Army Air Corps uniform and crouching next to a small child. He holds a white bunny by one foot like an offering as he gazes out from under his cap, smiling into the camera. The child, too, is smiling, almost laughing, her hand outstretched to touch the rabbit scrunched down into the grass, a small furry creature frozen by the camera, frozen into memory, waiting.

I am always struck by how happy I look in the picture. I search the child's face for a hint of what was to come, but all I see is trust as she leans against the khaki leg of the man who was my father for such a short time. I wonder if I waited for him by the big living room windows, watching for him to come back up the street, or if I went with my mother to the station to see him off again, standing on the platform while the steam rose around us, tasting metal in my smile. I wonder if I cried when he swung himself up the steps and disappeared inside the train. And I wonder why I can't remember.

Before we moved to Greenwood Street, my mother had a boyfriend named Henry, a little, dark haired man who always looked as if he were expecting bad news. My mother said he hadn't forgiven the world for delivering him into a Russian pogrom where his family had been so poor they were forced to search the streets for a piece of bread, and where Henry had grown up deformed. Lack of nutrition, she said, had given Henry a hunchback.

I liked Henry. He brought me little presents--a tiny chair for my doll house, or better yet, a hunk of halvah, a carton of shav, Russian soup made from sorrel or spinach. I loved the odd, spicy taste of Henry's food, but especially the soup. My mother said not many children liked this green soup, shaking her head at me in amazement while I ate it right out of the carton. She was completely indifferent to his food, as she was to all food, but Grandma hated it too.

And Grandma, I knew had affection for food. She'd fork the boiled potatoes with their tattered, hanging peels, pulling them from the pot dripping butter, calling them "taters" in a loving way, like you might nickname a favorite child. I saw the way she patted her plump loaves of oatmeal bread and carefully shaped her rolls, leaving them to rise in the steamy kitchen.

But Grandma hated Henry so much she didn't even like his presents. The thought of this ugly little man with her beautiful daughter drove her to distraction. "He's so short," she moaned. "What a shame for a lovely, tall woman to get stuck with a hunchback, a little pipsqueak of a man."

When my mother caught her whispering about Henry to me, she'd yell at her to "cut it out." But sometimes, grandma caught me outside my mother's range and whispered things like, "He's so ugly that if they ever marry, they'll have to put their children in a zoo."

I never defended Henry to her, never admitted I liked such an ugly person. And after Henry left, I'd stand in front of the hallway mirror and scrutinize my own sallow skin, as if there might be something Henry-ish about me. Something about his sad eyes reminded me of Grandma Sarah. I wished my skin were the color of peaches and my eyes china blue like Shirley Temple's.

In the afternoons on those crisp fall days of 1948, I went door-to-door with my mother among the gray stone apartment buildings in our neighborhood, campaigning for Henry Wallace. My mother said he was a "good man free from the corruption of big business." I liked campaigning. On those mornings, she tucked her dark hair under a black hat that made her skin even whiter and her eyes deeper. I loved wearing my good coat, walking along the street with my mother, feeling I was part of her work. I liked the excitement, the mystery of each new door. But most of all, I loved the food, because if they didn't shut the door in our faces, if they asked us in, I usually got fed.

When people we visited offered us food, my mother always politely turned it down, but I never did. Usually, it was some kind of sweet, or something even more sinful like shoestring potatoes, crisp with grease. At one house I ate the whole bowlful of them and then went home and threw up all over my bed. My mother cleaned up the bed, Henry took me to the bathroom to sponge me off and grandma came out into the hall and screamed at both of them. My mother threatened to stop taking me along if I couldn't control myself.

But the following week, there we were, sitting on the sofa in a strange living room, while my mother talked with the man of the house about campaign issues, and I stayed as quiet as possible waiting for the reward that was sure to come.

In the meantime, I got the chance to get a peek inside their lives. While the grown-ups' voices droned on, I sat trying to make myself invisible, while my eyes searched the stains on their furniture, scanned the books and magazines lying on the coffee table, and lingered on the family pictures hanging on their walls. I pictured them all together in this room, sisters and brothers lying carelessly about on the stained brown sofa eating candy and listening to the radio like we did in the evenings, only without the candy.

Then, just as I was beginning to get bored with the imagined family, the lady of the house would often come out of the kitchen in a gingham apron that smelled of cinnamon, look down at me, smile, and offer me a sliver of chocolate cake. It might be served on a white china plate trimmed with tiny rose buds. I'd hold the rich, chocolate taste in my mouth as long as I could before swallowing, letting the sugar seep into my tongue. I knew my mother wouldn't say no in front of them, especially when I smiled so sweetly and said, "Thank you very much."

My mother knew a political advantage when she saw one, and had to content herself by giving me a look that said, "You'll get Milk of Magnesia later."

When we got home, she lectured me about using "bourgeois manners," which meant saying things like "Yes, ma'am," and "Thank you." We never talked like this at home. My mother always said, "Honesty is the best manners you can have." But I knew her kind of honesty wouldn't get me another piece of cake, and besides, when I praised their cooking, I meant every word of it.

Sometimes, they'd ask as to dinner, but my mother drew the line there, taking it as a signal to leave. I would slide off my chair, sorry to leave the rich smells coming from the strange kitchen, while my mother pulled on her good black wool jacket, lifting her chin above the wool collar, her nostrils flared, alert to the scent of sugar. Then she took me by the hand and pulled me to the door. Outside on the street, she would say, "Honestly Christine, people will think we never feed you."

"But why *can't* we stay for supper?" I'd whine, already mourning the loss of a pot roast or a boiled chicken covered in gravy, grieving for the lost potatoes, whipped creamy smooth and dripping butter.

"We've no time to waste on food," she said in her brisk, cool voice. "There's too little time and too much work to do." And we would march together to the next house, with the air shimmering around us, brilliant in the afternoon sunshine.

While my mother waited to get a new President who would not "condone the policies of Harry Truman," the aunts came to visit. It would be the last time they were all together, and there was something in the way they pushed their bodies forward in their chairs when they resurrected the family ghosts, pressing themselves into each other, as if only talk could save them.

Aunt Marjorie came up from Texas. Nearly as tall as grandpa, with a deep voice and a stoop in her back, she brought my two cousins with her. Kiely, nearly three years younger than I, had curls like mine, only blond, and seemed like a baby to me. Cute but not very interesting. Her twelve year old sister, Christie, on the other hand, glided through our apartment--a goddess. My mother told me that as the oldest grandchild, she had gotten the family name, while I had to settle for "Christine."

Christie didn't pay much attention to me, but I spent a lot of time covertly watching her, wishing I could be so blasé, so grown-up. Once, she and a neighbor girl were allowed to take the streetcar all the way downtown by themselves. I watched from my bedroom door as they left the apartment with their purses tucked under their arms like matrons on their way to an important shopping trip.

Aunt Bee arrived a day or so later from New York. Bee lived, according to Grandma, in a penthouse apartment filled with brocade chairs and vases of roses. Originally called Mabel, after grandma's favorite cousin, Bee had re-named herself after the actress, Bebe Daniels, and the name had stuck with everyone, except my grandmother. My family seemed to have a propensity for name changes.

"Mabel's got a rich fella," Grandma said and winked at me like we shared a secret.

Tall and big boned, Bee had black hair and deep dimples that flashed when she smiled. She had a way of tightening a corner of her mouth so that at least one dimple winked even when her face was serious. They claimed she had the Christie voice and the Miles' white skin. "The beauty of the family," they all agreed. Then they narrowed their eyes and glanced over at me like they were afraid it might be catching. Grandma said my hair was as black as Aunt Bee's. But my mother said, "Don't put ideas in the child's head. Do you want her to grow up to live a life of beauty and despair?"

Grandma just sighed and went back to the kitchen.

But as far as I could see, Bee seemed to have the most fun. Perfume wafted from her black, clinging dresses, and she wore large brimmed hats with veils and pearls and had bright red fingernails and long, white fingers. The kind of hands my mother said looked "unused." Bee worked as a manicurist in New York, and she told us funny stories about the people who came into her shop. When she laughed, she threw her head back, and her laughter left echoes in the room. I adored her, but I was also a little jealous of her because I could see that my mother liked her, in spite of her remarks about Bee's delicate hands.

One day Aunt Bee took us into the music room, sat down on the piano stool and laid a white dish towel across her lap. Then she took my hand, holding it for a moment while she stared down at my fingers. "Such a tiny hand," she said, and her dimples winked at me. Then she got busy and painted my nails pink, the color of strawberry ice cream. Afterwards, she painted my mother's Poppy Red, and we all giggled. Then my mother became a younger sister, putting on some of Bee's lipstick. They bent their heads together and sparks flew out and around their soft hair, and their rich dark eyes danced the same bright dance.

The thing the Christie women liked to do best was sit around the dining room table screaming at each other and pretending to drink tea. Grandpa sat near-by in his big chair next to the radio and read the paper while they whooped and shouted. It seemed like he wasn't paying attention, but every now and then he interjected a comment into their conversation.

One day, I leaned up against my mother's lap day to get her attention, and asked why they were fighting all the time. They all stopped yelling and looked at me in surprise. "Why, we're not fighting, honey," said Aunt Bee, "that's just the way we talk." And in a minute, they were happily screaming at each other again.

They talked a kind of family shorthand, a hodgepodge of bits and pieces culled from family stories and quotes from the books they all read. I never could tell which pieces belonged to them and which belonged to other, better-known story tellers.

If, for instance, I came in from playing and needed a drink, my grandmother likely as not would say, "Water, water, everywhere and not a drop to drink," which actually meant, "I'm busy, so get it yourself." Another favorite of hers was, "The world is too much with us late and soon." This meant she was tired, or could also stand as an excuse for why something wasn't finished as in, "Oh, the world was too much with me today!"

My mother was fond of the Romantics, particularly Keats and Shelley and Blake, of course. But she could do Coleridge as well. Around Christmas, she liked to make up special arrangements:

Abu Ben Adam, may his tribe increase,
Awoke one day from a deep dream of peace,
and laying his finger aside of his nose,
and giving a shout, up the chimney he rose...

If I gave her a chance she would say it in front of my friends, who always looked bewildered and a bit shocked. "A Christmas carol," I'd explain. But I could tell they didn't really understand. I learned early on you had to be careful who you let in on some kinds of family talk.

That first night, after they lugged Aunt Bee's suitcases into the music room and found Aunt Marjorie's cigarettes, they headed immediately to the dining room table to chew over their lives. I followed them, knowing that if I kept quiet and pretended to be reading, they'd usually forget I was there. Aunt

Marjorie sat at one end of the table and took out her cigarettes. She sat with her head propped up on one hand as if it were too heavy to hold up without some help, and she held a cigarette in her other hand, which she mostly tapped in the ash tray. My grandmother sat next to her, smiling over at Marjorie from time to time, calling her "Marjorie-Peaches," her voice a kind of caress. Bee sat across from my mother with the teapot between them.

After they'd been at it for hours, Grandma got up and went out to do the dishes. I followed her and tried to dig out more information about Aunt Bee. "How come she smells like cotton candy?"

"That's because her boyfriend gave her a gallon of expensive perfume called Christmas Night."

"Where's her boyfriend?" I asked.

Grandma frowned and motioned with her head toward the dining room. "Shh." Her voice dropped into a loud whisper. "He's married. Now scoot. Your mother'll be mad if I say any more." And she sighed, and turned on the hot water. I didn't get it, so I went back out to the table to try to figure it out.

"God, we were miserable kids," I heard Bee say. She threw back her head, laughing like it had been such fun being miserable. Marjorie sat slumped even further down in her chair, furiously puffing on a cigarette.

"Bee! Quit that!" said Grandma coming in from the kitchen with the tea kettle and a plate of oatmeal cookies.

"Lickin's good, Sal," said Bee, and winked at her father who grinned back at her.

That expression came from a story Grandpa liked to tell about a guy from his home town back in Michigan who took his girl out riding in his horse and buggy one day and stopped for ice cream. He bought only one cone for himself, got back into the buggy and turned to his surprised girlfriend saying, "Lickin's good, Sal. Better buy you some."

Grandma began pouring steaming water into the pot. Her cheeks were flushed bright red from the heat. Bee looked down the table, our eyes met, and she gave me one of those flirty winks, like Grandma did sometimes for no apparent reason. "Your mother ever tell you about how she cried all night from ear infections?" Bee looked over at my mother who was rubbing the scar on her leg and gazing off into space. "*I'll* never forget hearing her crying half the night."

"Eve was the only one of our young'uns born in a hospital," said Grandma, "born during the blizzard of 1915, isn't that right, daddy?" That's what she called Grandpa when she wasn't mad at him, otherwise she called him "Clare" or the "old reprobate." He just nodded and spit into the tin can ready next to his chair.

"That's because the doctor said you weren't supposed to have any more babies," said Bee. "You were torn to shreds from Martin." My mother gave a warning nod in my direction. But Bee went on anyway. "Egads, when I think about the bloody sheets I washed while you lay there helpless as a lamb bleeding into a bucket..."

"Bee! The Child!" my mother's voice was adamant now.

Bee looked right at her and said, "The night you were born, I went out with mother while dad hitched the horses to the sleigh, and I said, 'this better be the last one. I'll run away if you have any more.'"

"I had them tie my tubes," said Grandma with a sigh. I had no idea what that meant, but it sounded final, like the way Grandma tied knots at the end of her embroidery thread. Grandma sat down again and was looking down at a piece of Kleenex she kept working around her fingers. "I did it for Mabel's sake. Poor thing, sick of all the babies."

"I should think you'd have done it for yourself, mother," said my mother, her lip curled back, signaling her disapproval.

"Oh she did, right Mocky?" said Aunt Bee, calling my grandmother by the nickname Grandpa gave her. Nobody seemed to know where he got it. My mother never used it, but her two older sisters did. Bee tapped her long, red nails on the table and smiled her wicked smile.

Grandma gave a sniff and lifted her chin at her daughters. "What could be more natural than babies? The more the merrier is what I always said, didn't I, daddy?"

I saw a look pass between the sisters. "I knew a girl in school," said Aunt Marjorie and her dark eyes gleamed with mischief, "who used to let the boys spit on her, and when we asked her why, she said, 'Natchally they spit.'" She threw back her head and laughed, the sound full and deep, sounding a lot like Marjorie, and they slapped their hands on the table in glee.

Grandma went right on ignoring her daughters. "If only those beautiful baby boys had lived, those precious babies..." and Grandma gave a long sigh, looking as if it happened yesterday, instead of forty years ago.

My mother sipped her tea now, not looking at anyone, as if she'd withdrawn herself from the memories. But I saw Marjorie and Bee exchange a look, and then Marjorie leaned into the table as if to command her mother's attention, and changed the subject.

"What I remember," said Marjorie, "is how Bee and I would take Eve out to that old house we made into our playhouse on Cook's Place. Martin would be upstairs having gun battles with his friends, and we girls would play all day out there. We even made curtains for the windows."

This was new to me because my mother always told me she didn't have any toys. I remembered when Grandpa said they had to hire a truck just to move all my toys to Greenwood Street, and my mother had shouted at him, "So what? At least she doesn't have to push a chair around pretending it's a doll buggy like I had to, with a pillow for a doll!"

"Yessiree, we had three grape arbors on Cook's place and an apple orchard," added Grandma, blowing her nose, her eyes dancing again.

"You left before the bottom dropped out," said my mother, looking at her older sisters.

"Did we?" Bee still smiled, but something pulled at the corners of her mouth.

"You and Marjorie were both in Detroit by the time the folks were losing everything," said my mother. "Living the glamorous life in the big city."

Aunt Marjorie snorted with disgust. "Gad! Some glamour all right! Bee made us get an apartment we couldn't afford in a "good" neighborhood, and we put the rest of our money on our backs. Didn't leave much for food." She reached back to wrap her long, brown hair more tightly around her head.

"Didn't matter," said Bee. "We could always make our dates take us out to supper."

"And you'd kick me under the table to remind me to eat enough to last," and Marjorie chuckled.

"What I remember," sighed my mother, beginning to put on her Little Match Girl face, "was when you two came home it always seemed like Christmas, and how I envied you because you had each other." Just like me, I thought, envious of my best friend Kay's brothers and sisters.

Grandma sighed and said, "Well, at least we always had fresh milk." She said fresh milk like she was saying filet mignon.

"The God damned oligarchy did me in," said Grandpa. "I never should have borrowed money to put in milking machines. But I didn't see how I had any choice. Couldn't make a living if I didn't sell to the condensed milk companies, and they insisted on the machines. That's what mortgaged me to the hilt."

"You had the cleanest milk in the county," said Grandma, indignation putting a snap in her voice. "Everyone knew that."

"Kept it together all during the worst times when other farmers were going under. Then lost it all anyway." He leaned down and spit into his can. "They stole my land and don't you forget it!" He gazed around the table at his daughters, to make sure they wouldn't, as if they ever could.

"You had politics, Eve," said Marjorie, smiling indulgently at my mother. "You wrote back to us and said we should both join the Proletarian Party because it was our duty "to relieve people."

"I remember," said Bee, "sounded like they had bowel problems." She whooped with laughter, waving her arms in glee. Later, I learned that Marjorie and Bee had been a part of a Detroit study group run by a young socialist minister named Reinhold Neibuhr.

I watched my mother's face. It had begun to change, to lose the Match Girl look, and she looked pleased with herself. "Dad said I could argue a crooked line straight," said my mother proudly. "Remember, how Martin and I spent our nights studying Marx together?" Aunt Bee rolled her eyes. Their only surviving brother, four years older than my mother, had still been on the farm with her.

"What a cozy scene. There we were, the typical American farm family, curled up with the one good light between us, whiling away the long winter nights fascinated by the words "surplus profit," thrilled by the idea of "class consciousness." They were all laughing now. "You bet," my mother shouted above the laughter, "we passed the volumes of *Das Kapital* between us, and it never occurred to us we were reading anything out of the ordinary."

"Remember that crazy man?" said Grandpa, "the one who had one arm and used to bang his stump at meetings."

"He banged it to wake us up after he put us all to sleep with his boring jargon," said my mother. "What I remember is the time he came out to the farm with a batch of leaflets for us to deliver. He handed them to me, then raised his stump and said, his voice dead serious, 'Here comrade, take these leaflets to the peasants.' God, he must've thought he was in pre-revolutionary Russia!" Even Grandma was laughing now, and Grandpa grinned and shook his head like he did when he was tickled.

"And to think Marjorie and I missed all that," said Bee, her dimples flashing. But my mother went right on. "All of us organizers wore bullet proof vests," she said. "Ted's car looked like a sieve from bullet holes."

Grandma sniffed. "I thought you were going to get yourself killed."

"Only once or twice," my mother said, and winked at her sisters. She was back in the territory she loved, the dangerous stories of her past glory. "I'll never forget my first job at Walgreens and my first organizing campaign for the newly formed C.I.O. We called a meeting at our store to try to get the employees interested in the new union, and the A.F. of L. sent in some thugs who tried to convince us not to join by standing in the back of the room, threateningly, arms folded, diamonds flashing on their pinkies. When the meeting ended, they called me over, all friendly and smooth as silk and offered me a ride home. But then suddenly, Martin was there, saying he'd take me home."

"Lucky for you," said Grandma.

"He had just started working for another Walgreens, and he came to see what was going on with the new union. But then he saw those guys with me. Not only did he take me home, but he made me get on and off streetcars and Els until I thought I'd drop from exhaustion, until he was sure they couldn't be following us. And all the way, he lectured me on how I was going to get myself killed if I didn't stop this dangerous union organizing."

It made me feel better in one way to hear how scared my uncle had been, like I wasn't the only coward, but it also made my fear more real, like something really might happen to my mother one day.

But the story made my mother's eyes dance, the way she always lit up when she talked about the dangerous times during the early days with the C.I.O., when union organizers were a renegade bunch who considered it a badge of honor to have bullet holes in their cars.

"Those were the days!" she said, looking blissful.

Aunt Bee chuckled. "I'll take a nice quiet race track any day."

"Yes. I loved to be right in the middle of the fray," said my mother, "loved knowing we were helping mankind take a great leap forward." Then she sighed the family sigh. "I just didn't see how I could go on being a good union organizer and a good mother too."

They all turned in my direction, and I felt suddenly nervous, even though I didn't really understand why.

Later, my mother would tell me her version of the story, the beginning of her fall from splendor. Then she would deliver it like a sermon, with virtue ringing in her voice. "There I stood, holding the telegram that offered me a top organizing position in the union, and there you were, still tiny and helpless, and I had to choose. And I did. I crumpled the telegram and threw it in the waste basket." Sometimes when she told this story, tears ran down her cheeks. Other times, her eyes grew radiant with her mother's choice, and she smiled brightly, grandly at her listeners.

"These days," she said now, "the country is drifting further and further to the right. A bunch of fascists calling themselves the House Committee on Un-American Activities seem to be in charge." Her voice automatically dropped in volume, as if F.B.I. agents lurked just beyond the door. "How dare they question the loyalty of good men and women who are guilty of nothing more than trying to help their fellow Americans get their democratic rights. What did we fight for in that damn war anyway, if not for democracy, and the rights of ordinary Americans? What did Mike die for, anyway?"

My ears perked up at the mention of my father. But everyone had been silenced. Even Bee sat hunched over her cold tea now. "Oh dear," said Grandma then. "But we've lived through some terrible times." And she looked around the room as if seeking confirmation.

Aunt Marjorie leaned over and patted my head, almost absently winding one of my curls around her long, bony finger as she spoke, her voice husky, bringing the memory of better times, "Remember how we'd troop back to the house at the end of the day in time to see dad coming in the wagon all heaped with corn or pumpkins?" They all watched her now, no one a bit surprised to be back suddenly on Cook's Place.

"And mother, you'd say, 'Our pumpkins are so large, Peter Pumpkin Eater could put in his whole family.' And then we'd all wait there together, Eve standing between us, waiting for dad to come over the hill from the back pasture. I can see him now, sitting tall in the wagon, the sun on fire behind him, and all around him fat, orange pumpkins. Mother would say to us, 'Life is real and life is earnest, but isn't it grand sometimes?' And we'd watch dad come toward us--it looked like from the very center of the sun."

They all sat silent now, joined by an invisible strand of sorrow, suspended in time together while I waited there at the table, my books forgotten, feeling it with them, this terrible loss, this last farm where my mother had been born, the one called Cook's Place, with the pastures flowing down to the creek, the apple orchards, all lost; the silos stacked high with grain, gone, the old frame house and the playhouse where little boys pitched gun battles and little girls played dress-up, all ruined; even the hay loft, where my father sat once and held my mother's hand in the soft light--all of it, gone forever.

After I was finally in bed, I could still hear their voices carrying down the hall far into the night, their shouts merging with their laughter. No one, it seemed, was allowed to leave until they all drooped over in their chairs from exhaustion. Usually when I got up in the morning, they'd be in the same places. I didn't think any of them slept at all. And before I fell asleep, I'd run through the scenes as if it were a home movie. I'd picture them as kids again in that lost farm kitchen with the tea kettle whistling on the cook stove, wishing I had a brother or sister to scream at all night long.

That fall, it seemed to me that one day I had been walking up the steps of my white frame nursery school on the University of Chicago campus with its back yard of cool, green grass, and the next minute I was enrolled in the public school surrounded by concrete. A tall metal fence guarded the cement playground, tall enough to keep children from escaping into the freedom of the streets. From the beginning, I had trouble. At my nursery school, a lab school for the university, I had been treated with affectionate delight, much as I was at home. But the public school showed only indifference towards the children.

As far back as I could remember, I had been treated as a person to be dealt with in a serious manner. When I was still so short that I stood about even with my grandfather's lap, I came into the dining room one evening to tell him something. He was sitting in his easy chair with the one good lamp shining down on his paper, and he took issue with what I said. I must have argued back. He put down his paper, looked at me over the rims of his glasses and said, "Christine, your logic is faulty. Go back and rethink your arguments." I went to my bedroom, where my mother was smoothing the covers on my bed. "Doesn't he realize," I said, "that I'm only four years old?"

So it was like being in a foreign country, this place where children were lined up and made to march in silence into the classroom, where they sat in rows of hard, brown desks, silently, where quiet ruled with the iron hand of a teacher who never smiled, but rather, sat at her desk, hands folded in front of her and glowered at us.

The torment started almost the minute I left our apartment and made my way down the long street into the alien world where sturdy, straight-haired blond children knew secrets that I would never know--what kind of boots to wear on their skipping feet, careless with their steps, or the kind of coat, the popular colors--blue or brown, not black like the one my mother had bought at a Marshall Field's basement sale. It was the kind of coat Aunt Bee in New York would love, she had reassured me, but I didn't care about that. I wanted a purely Chicago coat. And a real Chicago hat, not like the green one with round red balls of yarn all over it that my mother pulled down over my ears, the one that made the kids call out, Christine-Ice-cream-With-Cherries-On-Top, a chant that sent me home head down, fighting tears.

Years later, my mother would tell me that every time she rubbed Vasoline into my chapped lips, it broke her heart. It was too much like her own miserable childhood as a farm kid bullied by the city kids.

But back in Chicago, she had tried to make me brave by inciting me to riot against my tormenters. "Beat them up!" she'd exhort me. But I could not even raise my head in my own defense. My skinny neck wouldn't bear the weight, my long thin hands withdrew inside my coat sleeves, my shoulders slumped, my chest caved inward, my face turned pinched and yellow. I imagined I must look wizened, wrapped up in all that wool like a mummy.

These kids on the playground at this new school even carried their bodies differently. They seemed comfortable in their skin, shoulders back, chests stuck out like I imagined my mother must have done back in Michigan when she had beaten up the snotty town kids who called her names.

Where, I wondered, did you learn toughness? Was it something that could be taught like arithmetic, or were you just born with it like blond hair or stocky legs? Or was it fathers, or sisters and brothers who taught this important information that allowed you to be comfortable in the world? And if I couldn't be comfortable, my mother seemed to expect me to be fearless. But no matter how many times my grandmother said, "'Can't' never did anything," I could not affect this attitude, could not feel easy. I hadn't yet hardened. That would come much later, after life had required me to shape-shift on a regular basis, and I would learn to solidify quickly into anything that allowed me to survive. But for now, I seemed to be, in my mother's words a "mewling baby," or according to my grandfather, "a namby-pamby."

My grandmother could only whisper, "Remember, God-loves-little-children." That did nothing but confirm my suspicions that her God was indifferent to my childish pain.

"Only fools are never afraid," Grandpa would remind me, "being brave means being afraid and doing it anyway." I sort of felt included in that advice because every morning I struggled into the unwanted coat, the hated hat, my lips chapping almost the instant I stepped out into the grime of the streets and made my way carefully, like picking a path across a mine field down the long streets, through the gray Chicago morning toward the dreaded building, lurking in shadows in the distance, like a prison, dark and forbidding, marooned in an island of concrete.

At home, I whined and complained, sitting at the kitchen table, pouting while my mother made me eat oatmeal for strength, begging to return to my old school. She stood at the stove, still in one of her morning outfits, an old tee shirt covered by even older flannel pajamas under a faded chenille robe. She lectured about "doing my duty." "I don't want you to grow up to be a snob," she told me.

"But I'm not," I protested, "How would I get to be a *snob* when I don't even know what one *is*?"

She paused in the act of pouring oatmeal into my bowl and regarded me sadly. "I want you to grow up with the children of the men and women who work in plants, not the children of university professors." She spit out the words *university professors* with disdain, the way Grandpa said *bosses*. It was confusing to me because I knew that Kay's father worked at the university, and she liked him, but I also knew they were not in the inner circle of friends with serious faces who sat in our living room at night for meetings, or the people in blue work clothes I met at union halls.

There was nothing to do but accept it. Still, I sulked and dabbed at the grey blobs floating around in my milk, hardly able to push the spoon past my chapped lips. "You've gotta be brave," she said. "Just think how I had to walk five miles to school through blizzards every day with nothing to eat but cream pie!"

I thought cream pie sounded a lot better than oatmeal, but when I said so, she just got more worked up. "Be thankful you don't have some maniac teaching you, like the one who humiliated me when I wet my pants and made me stand at the stove in front of the class all day while they dried."

Talk about me, I wanted to shriek. *I'm the one who's suffering now!* But she was only getting warmed up. Her movements at the stove grew firmer, and the pans began to clatter ominously in the background as her voice rose above the clatter, claiming my attention.

"Be glad for heat! We froze all winter. My hands got so chapped they cracked, and I couldn't get them clean, and the city kids laughed at us farm kids. I beat up one snotty little girl so often they had to send her home early." She laughed with angry pleasure and banged the oatmeal pot on the table in front of me, making me jump like she'd hit me. Then she wound up for the grand finale, dropping her voice to a dramatic whisper. "It'd be dark by the time I left for home, dark and cold and lonely, and I'd think if I can just make it over this next hill, then I'll be safe, and I'd keep saying that to myself the whole long, cold five miles! I don't know how I stood it! So be thankful!"

By this time, I'd be feeling sorry for her, but resentful just the same. I wished everyone in my family didn't always have a worse story, a more terrible affliction to bear.

One night, I opened the front door and saw a strange man standing there. He looked startled to see me, and his face went pink all the way back to his hairline. But then his eyes smiled at me through his glasses, and he said, "Hi, I'm Walter. Is Eve home?" And just like that I knew my father had come to dinner. We ate scrambled eggs because my mother did the cooking that night, and eggs were the only things she knew how to fix, along with string beans, and she forgot to break off the ends, so everyone spent the meal picking them out of their teeth. I watched Walter to see how he was taking this, but he didn't say much, just smiled a lot and picked out bean ends.

But Walter didn't fit my father fantasy. Too short and too quiet to be related to me, I thought. He just didn't make a very convincing hero. But even Grandma liked him. I remembered how much she hated my mother's old boyfriend, Henry. He had been short, too, a dark-haired man who always looked like he was expecting bad news. The thought of this little, man with her lovely daughter drove her to distraction. "He's so ugly," she told me, "if they ever marry they'll have to put their children in a zoo." I never defended Henry, never admitted I liked such a homely person, and sometimes, after Henry left, I'd stare at my wiry, curly hair and my sallow skin and wonder if there was something Henryish about me.

"Walter's a sweet and gentle man," she told me one afternoon while I stood next to her in the kitchen, watching her make oatmeal bread, "a blond." She said the word *blond* with delight, almost licking her lips over the idea.

"But he's short," I reminded her. "You don't like short people."

"What of it. He's a good man. You just wait and see."

I stood there, watching her shape the rolls, rubbing margarine onto the tops before laying them in the aluminum baking pan. But I remained unconvinced.

In December, Walter and my mother became engaged, but not much in my life changed. I still hung around my grandparents, and my mother still tucked me in bed at night. Then one night just as I was getting my pajamas on and saying goodnight to my sick dolls, I heard Grandma cry out, "Mabel!" and then, "Clare! Come quick!" When I came into the hall where the phone sat on the small, wood table, Grandma stood there with one hand over her heart. Grandpa had already come into the hall to stand beside her. "What is it?" I asked. But Grandma shushed me and said, "It's from New York!" It was nearly unimaginable to be getting a call from New York, far-away place where people walked around bathed in perfume and furs, that place where Aunt Bee lived.

My mother rushed down the hall, and Grandma handed her the phone. We stood in a cluster--waiting, and when she put down the phone, her face had changed. She started smoothing my curls back from my face with her fingers, in the way she did when she was worried about something. Then she told us Aunt Bee had been taken to the hospital with pneumonia. Grandma immediately began to cry and to ask God for help. And no one told her to stop being silly like they usually did when she talked to God. My mother made plane reservations.

While my mother was in New York, Aunt Bee died in the hospital of bulbar pneumonia, and my mother stayed to clean up my aunt's affairs. While she was gone, Walter moved more firmly into our lives. We made pancakes together in the mornings, and now Walter read me my bedtime story, but he didn't take on the voices of the characters like my mother did. When I asked him to snuffle like Pooh, he tried, but it came out more like a hiccup than a snuffle. After he left the room, I cried myself to sleep. If he heard me crying, he came to the door and said, "She'll be home soon," while I pretended to be comforted and squeezed down further under the covers. I missed my mother's voice; his voice startled me coming through the dark bedroom, a strange man's voice, cheerful and cool, not the voice of a bass drum, the voice of my real father. And no matter what they all told me, I was convinced my mother was never coming back. And in a way I was right.

When my mother returned, she did three unprecedented things: she brought home a silver fox coat of Bee's which she insisted on wearing to demonstrations and picket lines. She tossed her head impatiently when anyone mentioned the expensive coat and said, "Maybe they'll listen harder to us if they think we have some money. I'm tired of progressive people looking like they're totally poverty-stricken when they're not." She also took a part-time job in her old union office doing the office work she'd always disliked, and she and Walter got married.

That shouldn't have changed things much, since Walter had been living in the apartment while my mother was in New York. But things felt different. She still read me my bedtime story, but she had stopped doing her interpretive dancing, and even though I had once found it embarrassing, now I tried to pull her back into it. But she'd mutter," Not right now, honey," and then go around the apartment looking distracted, as if she were listening for something in the next room. But except for that night when the call came, when grandma cried out "Mabel!" and put her hand over her heart, I didn't see their grief over my aunt's death at all. Grief always entered my life through the back door, sneaking in so quietly I never heard it, never had time to prepare, to protect myself from the invasion. I didn't even recognize it until it was too late, and it had already brought a new life, one that I never asked for; one that I never wanted.

One night during supper, my mother read a newspaper editorial calling one of her union co-workers, a "lean and hungry Cassius." It went on to say that he was a dangerous man "capable of manipulating politics to further the plans of Communism."

"My God," she said, shoving the paper angrily onto the table, "Herb was courted by the government when they wanted the unions to help create a united work force for the war effort. Now that unemployment is high again and workers are afraid to make demands, they think don't need us anymore. Big business is going to snap up the chance to get rid of the progressives."

"Are we a progressive?" I asked.

"Of course we are," said my mother. "Just like any intelligent, decent person."

But that did nothing to allay my uneasiness, and it didn't help that Grandpa shook his head silently over the pile of food on his plate. He always moved his mashed potatoes and carrots into pie shaped portions, and then cut them into careful wedges before eating them slice by slice.

One day my mother came home from the union office and stormed out to the kitchen where Grandma was boiling potatoes and Grandpa sat at the kitchen table reading the papers. I heard her tell them that Herb's son Bob had been tormented on the playground by other students who had called his dad "a dirty Commie." Bob had to run with the pack after him until he caught a passing streetcar. I remembered that my mother had said *they* would "try to get rid of *us*." If we were like Herb's family, then the same thing could happen to me.

I felt even less safe on my school playground after that--the flat gray cement seemed to go on forever, open and dangerous. At recess, I found a nice brick corner of the building to hide in, out of view from the rest of the playground, a kind of refuge. It afforded me privacy so that I didn't have to feel so naked, so exposed, out in the open on the playground in front of the other kids. No one seemed to miss me. Standing there morning after morning, running my hands over the brick, it began to take on life. I could almost feel it breathing beneath my fingers. And I would whisper, "Good morning" to it, calling my corner Reddy as if it were a real live flesh and blood friend, telling it stories, standing there in the quiet spring sunshine, while the playground noise rose in the distance, feeling almost safe against the red brick.

I developed a stutter that winter, especially in class whenever I tried to talk, so I tried to say as little as possible. I stopped saying the words of the Pledge of Allegiance. I still stood every morning, pretending to say it like everyone else, even though my family treated this kind of patriotic display with disdain. Grandpa always said saluting the flag was "like saluting big business."

A boy from my classroom started following me home, calling me,"Christine-ice-cream-with-cherries on-top" because of the silly hat covered with red pompoms.

When I complained to my mother, I could tell she didn't take it very seriously. "Think of how they went after poor little Bob," she said. But I saw little difference between "dirty Commie" and "Cherry-ice-cream." I saw myself singled out, a possible target of something more awful that waited just around the street corner to get me. I came home every day with chapped lips, where all my fears had congealed and stiffened.

Nearly every night for the rest of that school year, the sheet ghost waited at the edges of my dreams to follow me until I forced myself awake. I lay there in bed and scrunched my eyes tight, so I could picture my father riding toward me on a fiery red horse, galloping across the sheet, one hand grasping the thick mane, and the other swinging free, ready to swoop down and grab me, ready to lift me up and carry me away to another place, where I would be safe forever.

California was only a sound without any meaning to me when my family started talking about going there. Grandma muttered about "soon being out of this filthy place." And "Soon, we'll be in Californ-I-A." She had always talked about the "city dirt," but there wasn't any real venom behind the words. Now, it sounded like she couldn't wait to leave.

I couldn't imagine actually *leaving* Chicago, actually *living* anywhere else. "A new beginning," my mother said, "a new life."

But I didn't want a new life. I didn't understand why the old one wasn't good enough. And I wondered what would happen to all the sick dolls. Who would care for them? I couldn't imagine not bouncing my ball on the sidewalk outside the apartment buildings, or playing cowboys in the mud yard out in back, or the Saturday afternoon movies, or even the friends who sat in our living room for meetings; these were the people who made up my world.

But sometime that spring, my grandparents left Chicago first, leaving so quietly the memory got muffled, leaving an empty space. Even now, there is a part of me that does not want to believe in the rest, to remember the new lives that came after. Instead, I want to remember us perpetually moving through the rooms of that Chicago apartment, warm with the scent of oatmeal bread, and the sweet, stale smell of tobacco scrunched inside a sweaty shirt pocket. My grandmother's laughter echoes down the hall, her pumps clicking on the linoleum as she moves through the tasks of her day. She passes my grandfather in his easy chair, and she pauses, then leans down to kiss the top of his bald head shining in the lamplight above him.

The day we left Chicago, I stood in front of the glass doors and took a last look, scanning the sunny street for signs, then turning to look back up the stairs as if I could penetrate the dark and find a way back up to our old life. Then my mother called for me to hurry, and when I turned and went past the mailboxes, I saw our names had already been removed. There wasn't even our pretend name any more. Then I went out the door and got into the car, scrunching in between the bags of last minute stuff my mother had crammed in along with clothes for the trip. She turned around in the seat, smiled her jaunty, let's-try-to-be-brave kind of smile and said, "We're off to sunny California."

"It's sunny in Chicago," I muttered.

"You'll see," she said.

I scrunched down in the seat and tried not to look at the quiet sidewalk, or think about my best friend Kay, in school without me. Walter put the car in gear, and we lurched down Greenwood Street, on our way to a new life, one that I never asked for, one that I never wanted.

McCarthy sprang to national prominence in February, 1950 with a speech at Wheeling, West Virginia, during which he claimed to be holding in his hand a list of 205 Communists employed by the State Department...

In California, Richard M. Nixon, having red-baited the New Dealer and former Socialist Jerry Voorhis out of the House in 1946, now employed the same tactics to defeat Democratic Congresswoman Helen Gahagan Douglas for the Senate in 1950. He issued a pink sheet showing how Mrs. Douglas's voting record paralleled that of New York's Vito Marcantonio (who invariably voted the CP line) on 354 occasions. Nixon won by nearly 500,000 votes...

...an Official Referee(Frank J. Gregg) could in 1950 grant a woman (Mrs. Maria careccia, an annulment of her marriage solely on the grounds that her husband was a Communist...

David Haute, *The Great Fear*

When in 1950, Republicans sponsored an Internal Security Act for the registration of organizations found to be "Communist-action" or "Communist-front," liberal Senators did not fight that head on. Instead, some of them including Hubert Humphrey and Herbert Lehman, proposed a substitute measure, the setting up of detention centers (really concentration camps) for suspected subversives, who when the President declared an "internal security emergency" could be held without bail.

Howard Zinn, *The People's History of the United States*

Different families handled it in different ways. Dalton Trumbo said of his children, "It is impossible for a child to live thirteen or fourteen years in the house of a blacklisted, disgraced, jailbird writer and not be affected by it. We did everything we could to ameliorate the wounds that did occur...
-Victor S. Navasky, *Naming Names*

I couldn't care less if they were investigated as Communists or not," said [Country Joe] McDonald, who grew up in southern California, "all I cared about was when I went to a Cub Scout meeting or went to play baseball...I didn't feel comfortable anymore.
-Dana Kennedy, The folks were reds: documentary film traces lives of American communists' children, Associated Press.

On July 17, 1951, Julius Rosenberg was arrested as a spy. On August 11, Ethel Rosenberg was also arrested. They left behind two small sons.

California, 1949-1950

We drove for days across hot, dry plains that went by in a blur of light through the windows. My mother refused to drive, which was odd because she was the one who taught Walter to drive before we started this trip. Now, she stared dully out of the window as if the blowing dust and the empty plains frightened her, while I chatted at her from the back seat.

Walter kept telling us we were both missing the "once-in-a-lifetime scenery." Occasionally, I stopped talking and tried to picture real cowboys out there riding horses and twirling their lassoes above their heads. But that got boring, since I wasn't allowed to imagine them pulling their guns and shooting. "No violence," my mother said. "If we want peace, we have to *imagine* it first."

In Chicago, when my friends and I had played cowboys and Indians in our apartment, my mother tried to get us to let the Indians kill all the cowboys. She embarrassed me by telling everyone, "*We* stole this land from the Indians," her voice loud and insistent like it got when she made speeches. I took the role of Indian, the only acceptable role according to my mother, and Barbara, who always played a cowboy, shook her blond curls and muttered, "Your mother is weird." Probably, I thought, the only reason they kept playing at my house anyway was because we could chase through our apartment and use the furniture for hideouts. Now, I was finding the real West a lot less exciting than our games had been.

A couple of days into the trip, we stopped at a fake ranch where huge stuffed animals posed for the tourists with their backs hunched and their legs kicking. Walter got out the camera and insisted I sit on top of a bucking steer to get a picture for my grandmother. Then he lifted me up, and someone handed me a cowboy hat, which I held in one hand while I grasped the saddle horn with the other. The fake fur, all stiff and matted, prickled my fingers when I grabbed the cow's fake backbone because I felt dizzy being up so high off the ground.

I remembered when Grandpa drew stick cowboys, he always told me how bad they stank. "Think of it," he said, "riding all day under the broiling sun, and then sleeping in dirty, flea ridden bed rolls, no bath, no nothing for days on end." I hadn't believed him, but now sitting up on top of the phony beast, I could smell a faint musty odor, like it might really have fleas.

After we got back on the road, my mother tried to entertain me like she always did by telling stories. She made up a long saga about a character called Wild Bull Hiccup who stank up the West in his dirty underwear and refused to use his gun, no matter what. The story irritated me, but I was used to nobody killing anyone in my mother's stories, or else she got it backwards like with the cowboys and Indians, or she left out the parts she called "racist," sometimes tearing whole pages out of my story books, and the story ending up not making much sense.

In between stories, she and Walter talked in quiet voices, while I drifted in and out of the conversation.

They worried about the people who had been their friends back in Chicago who had lost union jobs. My mother told Walter this "whole thing was a bunch of cold war nonsense." And when I asked her what that meant, she turned around in her seat, her face red from the heat and said in a hard voice, "It means Truman and the boys in Washington are nasty red baiters, calling good people names." She turned back to Walter. "Can you believe the papers are calling Dorothy Healy "The Red Queen"?

I didn't really understand what it all meant, but the name intrigued me. "Do we know Dorothy Healy? I asked.

"She lives in California. We don't exactly *know* her, but she's one of our people."

Part of the club, I thought, like the people who came to our apartment in Chicago to meetings and sat around all night talking about the "issues."

Then my mother said, "They're trying to discredit all the leaders and destroy the union movement, or anything resembling progressive thought in this country." Her voice had grown too loud for the car. "It looks like they're going to do to everyone what they did to Herb." Walter just shook his head and didn't say anything.

But I remembered when Herb's son, Bob, had been surrounded on the playground and had to run for the bus.

"Whatever happened to Bob?" I asked.

"Happened?" But she had forgotten about little Bob already, and she went on in her loud, speech making voice. "What a country that makes martyrs out of its heroes!" She began to sing one of her favorite union songs:

"When the union's inspiration through the worker's blood shall run,
There can be no power greater anywhere beneath the sun,
Yet what force on earth is weaker than the feeble force of one,
For the union makes us strong.
Solidarity Forever,
For the union makes us strong…"

But I was daydreaming. It should have been a Palomino that rescued him instead of a bus, or a red horse, like the Strawberry Roan in the song Grandpa used to sing. In my story, I would turn the bus into a strawberry roan, and I would ride with my father who would be wearing a cowboy hat and spurs, sitting tall in the saddle. We'd ride off together through the sagebrush in a cloud of dust.

"Maybe we got out of the Midwest in time," my mother said, her voice heartened by the singing. "It looks like things are heating up quick."

Sweating in the back seat as we hurtled across the plains on our way to join the "Red Queen" in California, I could only wonder what could be worse than this because already I missed Kay and hated our new life. I took long, dreamy naps, and when I awoke the boring West still flashed by outside the car windows.

When we crossed the mountains, my mother lay down on the back seat, and I got to sit in front, but then she started worrying about me being too vulnerable up there and made me squeeze onto the seat with her while Walter rode all alone up front. He tried to point out that if we went off the mountain it probably wouldn't make much difference where I was sitting because the fall would be about the same. But she moaned and said if he wasn't still, she was going to vomit.

Luckily, it got dark finally, and she got quiet, and I think she fell asleep. Later, she always said she had to "get drunk and lie on the floor of the car." And maybe she did. All I knew was the dry grass, the color of mustard went on and on, and I kept feeling our real lives, the ones we had left behind in Chicago unraveling and slipping away.

At last we drove down a street in the suburb of Compton, Ca. and stopped, and I, feeling as hot and sticky as one of those mythical cowboys, pressed my face to the window and saw that the streets sparkled. Even the cement seemed to come in colors with tiny diamonds embedded in its surface. I looked beyond the sidewalk to a yellow brick walk like a magic path, winding through the lawns and lined on both sides with yellow roses. A white stucco house, set back from the street was snuggled in the lush California green. I was dazzled by the colors and stunned by the silence. The noisy Chicago streets receded as we stepped out into the hush of El Segundo Boulevard.

And then Grandma came out of the front door, hurrying down the walk, and I pushed away the strangeness, leaped out of the back seat and threw myself into her arms, "You're home, little darling," she whispered against my hair, and some tightness I had been holding in since we left Chicago loosened a little.

But we didn't join the "Red Queen." Quickly, the name receded into the distant past of our old life because in our new life in California, everyone seemed different-more energetic. Grandma ran the house like before, her kitchen redolent with the smell of bleach from washing dishpans of vegetables, she brought in from the kitchen garden just outside the back door.

My grandfather didn't have time to tell Baddy Boy stories. Instead, he started his days early tending the garden or the fruit trees that stretched out to the end of our land. Walter was going to school to get his PH.D. and substitute teaching, and my mother didn't go off to a union office. But she seemed busier than ever working with the carpenters who were re-doing one of two small rental cottages that took up part of our back acre. She went around in old jeans, muttering about "square footage" and "ceramic tile," a whole new vocabulary of building words.

She and Walter even joined a group that did square dancing, dressing in long., colorful dresses that Grandma helped her sew. They danced in our living room, the men do-se-doing in cowboy boots, and the women twirling round and round, their skirts dipping gracefully to the music. She seemed like a new person. "Nonsense," she said when I told her she seemed different, "I've always loved to dance." But it wasn't the dancing exactly that made the difference, more like the frivolity of this new life. For the first time, her activities were unconnected to some higher ideal. Our family life seemed more normal now. The grownups were busy doing "real" work and not so much reciting verses or telling stories.

Although Grandma could still be counted on to recite Tennyson over the dishpan, and "when splendor falls on castle walls" took on new meaning for me.

As for me, gradually the dazzle of the flowers and the green yard began to penetrate. I noticed the earth smell and the smell of sunshine. I leaned to pay attention to them, not just to push away the bad smells, but to welcome them as messages. My new bedroom at the back of the house, a converted porch really, led out into the yard, and my grandmother's cat Annie became my friend, sleeping out there, curled up next to me at night.

In the morning, I scrambled out of bed, maybe throwing on the same old rumpled clothes, and made my way passed Grandpa already out digging in his garden while Annie kept watch over gopher holes. My feet became callused, my skin turned reddish brown, and my hair tangled.

I learned to notice how some trees spread out their limbs invitingly, while others turned their limbs into leafy rooms. I ate peaches for breakfast, and settled myself between the branches where I could see above the houses and down the sunlit street listening to the quiet, broken only by the clunking sound of Grandpa's hoe beneath me.

I climbed the rough trunks, with newly calloused feet, going higher and higher, until Grandma watching from the window would put down the dish towel, run out into the yard and yell, "Stop."

She caught her breath at the sight of me up in the trees, calling out, "Must you go so high?" And I went even higher until she had to go inside because she couldn't watch. For the first time, I felt myself to be beyond harm, and I stopped sleeping with the light on at night.

Later, I would feel those early months in California when the family, including my cousins, gathered often in Grandpa's little orchard to eat fruit, and listen to the grown-ups fight old childhood battles and talk politics, that this had all been a trick, had lulled me into thinking we were safe. I cannot remember any picnic in any of the other places that came later, not a beach, a park, nor even an open field where they might have spread a cloth down on the grass and sat together in the sunshine

I would learn to be more vigilant, to listen for any disturbance in the atmosphere around me because it could happen so softly. Trouble, I would learn, could begin with just a murmur in the air, a whisper like the rustle of wings.

Sometime in that first summer, we had a kind of picnic out in the yard in back of the house. The grownups sat at the picnic table in the yard talking to each other like they usually did while my cousin Karen and I rode around the yard on fast horses, brandishing our six shooters in the air, or pointing them at her little sister Patsy who didn't make a very satisfying bad guy. After we had chased her for a few minutes, her pale hair hanging in limp strands over her eyes, she got tired of playing the victim and stopped running. "You can't stop," yelled Karen, her voice shrill with indignation. "You've got to try to get away!" But Patsy took a breath, clenched her fists, screwed up her eyes and screamed.

Karen and I retreated to the orchard to build a ranch house out of old crates. When we saw Patsy coming through the trees toward us, Karen narrowed her eyes. Patsy's fine hair had been pulled back with a barrette and the tears washed from her face. Her face had a streak of dirt down one cheek, the front of her shirt was covered with burrs. She kind of meandered along towards us through the trees humming a song to herself. Karen called out, "Hey Pat, wanna play? You can be on our side." Then Karen leaned toward me and whispered, "She can be the cattle we're rustlin'." Patsy smiled her shy smile and for a second, I felt guilty. For a few minutes we all whooped and shouted and darted between the trees, but then Karen called out, "Now!" and we turned Patsy into a renegade steer, lassoed her and tied her to an almond tree. She started shrieking again, so Karen and I climbed a neighboring peach tree, so we could peek through the branches and safely watch the fireworks.

This time, Uncle Martin and my mother came over to see what we had done to her. "Here. Here," Uncle Martin said as he untied his daughter. She buried her face against him while he awkwardly patted her head. People always made a fuss over

Patsy's fine, blond hair. Once, I heard Grandpa say she had hair "like an angel."

My mother was wearing her carpenter pants, and she had tied her hair back with a scarf. She wasn't wearing much make-up these days and her smooth face made her look like a boy. She stood there frowning while Uncle Martin patted Patsy. "Seems to me," she said, "your oldest daughter resembles you picking on *your* little sister."

Uncle Martin turned toward my mother, biting the side of his cheek like Aunt Bee used to do, but instead of making a deep dimple, it pulled at his long, narrow face, and gave his mouth a curious dip on one side. "How come you never remember any of the good things I did for you?"

"Like what?" asked my mother.

"What about the time you set yourself on fire, "and I saved your damn life by rolling you outside in the snow."

"You were probably going that way," said my mother.

"See?" He threw up his hands in a mock gesture of despair. "According to you, I'm a scoundrel."

They had both forgotten poor Patsy who stood there rubbing her eyes and hiccupping.

"How about when you chased me with the butcher knife?" asked my mother.

"Oh come on." He gave a kind of chuckle. "You always exaggerate!" They both somehow looked happy instead of mad, excited to be out here fighting old, familiar fights again. This was beginning to remind me of our old life in Chicago when they stayed fixed in the past all day.

Then my mother turned and looked up into the peach tree. "You two are going to miss the rhubarb pie if you're not careful."

She and Uncle Martin started back toward the others, forgetting all about Patsy. Uncle Martin kept trying to get my mother to "remember one, just one good thing." Patsy ambled along in back of them. "C'mon Patsy," said my uncle, impatience in his voice, "don't diddle-daddle."

I could hear my grandparents in the distance, and my mother called out, "C'mon everyone. I'll show you the stairway to heaven."

We could hear them all moving off toward the back cottage, and after a minute, Karen and I climbed down and followed them. When we reached the front door, they were all standing in the living room which smelled of fresh cut pine, and my mother was showing off her "triumph," the new, free standing staircase. She had talked the carpenters into building it after she read about it in a magazine. Grandpa had stood around shaking his head and saying it wouldn't work. But there it was glowing in the afternoon sun coming in through the tiny window she had them build above it. The sun warmed the wood to a rich, caramel color, smooth as satin. Little spirals of light illuminated the stairs that rose straight up from the floor, straight up into the light. Grandpa pushed his hat back on his head and grinned over at my mother who stood with her hands in her pockets looking up the stairway, her face triumphant in the sunlight.

Later, my mother sat at the rough wooden table, eyes flashing like they used to back in Chicago when she came home from a day of union organizing, looking like she might take off at any moment while she told everyone about learning to fly planes. "Just think!" she said, "When I get my license, we can go anywhere, around the world if we want. There'll be nothing to stop us."

Uncle Martin smiled his crooked smile, and lazily cut oranges into a glass bowl.

And I, sitting on the stoop with my cousins, the air thick and sweet with the smells of summer, was content to lie back on my elbows, feel the warm dirt between my toes and remember the story I had heard Aunt Marjorie tell back in Chicago about standing with her sisters watching Grandpa bringing in the magic pumpkins on their lost farm.

It began to grow dark, and still we sat together, my cousins and I, our arms almost touching, our fingers sticky with fruit juice, our bodies lazy in the warm dusk while the grown-ups talked on and on and forgot it was passed our bedtime. "Karen" I whispered, "wouldn't it be great if we could just freeze everyone?"

"You mean like when we play statue?"

"Yeah. Just call out freeze, and we'd all stay forever, just like we are now."

"We might get tired of it. We might want to change to something else."

"I wouldn't," I said. And I meant it.

One evening early in the winter of 1950, Walter and I were playing Crazy Eights at one end of the dining room table while my mother and grandfather studied navigation charts together at the other end, Grandma sat in the reading chair darning socks. I was busy trying to figure out a way I could cheat without Walter catching on, when the phone rang. At first, no one moved. Here in our new life, the phone hardly ever rang. My mother had been too busy learning carpentry and taking flying lessons, and except for the square dance club, they hadn't made many friends. Walter put his cards down and answered it. Then he said, "Who is this?" Something sharp in his voice caught my attention, and I noticed my mother looked up from the table as well. After another few moments he said, "You must be referring to our work in the Progressive Party and the Wallace campaign."

That sounded like political talk, so I got busy trying to peek at his cards while he was clearly distracted. Then he said, and now his voice had a harder edge. "Before the campaign, I was serving my country in the army. Do you want to talk about that?"

I glanced over at my mother and saw that she had closed her book and was sitting very still, her eyes fixed on Walter's face as if she could hear better that way. Suddenly, the atmosphere in the room had shifted, tension palpable in the air. Grandma had dropped her darning into her lap, and she and Grandpa watched my mother, as if the message would come through her.

Walter spoke in a hard voice I had never heard him use before. "Look, if I've done something wrong, come and arrest me. Otherwise, leave me alone. I have nothing to say to you, now or ever!" He hung up the phone and looked over at my mother, sitting very still, the book forgotten on her lap.

"Well," my mother said taking a long, shuddering breath. "It's begun."

For me, it began with the Devil Bat's daughter. Over the next weeks, our lives continued in the usual way. Then one day after dinner was over, and we had drifted into the dining room where we usually played cards, Walter didn't get out the deck. In fact, he sat in his usual chair, quieter than usual and didn't go near the cards. Instead, he just sat there smoking a cigarette until finally, he looked up at my mother and said, "It seems they don't need anyone to substitute teach in that wretched school with its barbed wire fence like a concentration camp. And you know that's a lot of bull when they were begging for teachers a few weeks ago."

My mother looked up from the paper and shook her head but didn't say anything. After a few minutes of paging through the paper, she said, "Here's one. 'Cocktail waitress wanted for a new country western restaurant.'" She frowned. "What do you suppose country and western actually means?"

"Cowboys and cowgirls," I said.

My mother looked up at me over the paper and grimaced. "Maybe I'll have to wear a six shooter and spurs to work."

I thought that sounded great, but my mother didn't look too happy.

But she got the job. The restaurant was way out in Beverly Hills, decorated in what my mother called "phony old west." She complained about everything, the traffic jams on the way to work, about having to turn her square dance dresses into uniforms, about the business men who came in to lunch on t-bone steaks. "Can you imagine a pound of steak at lunch!" she said aghast. "And they're all overweight already."

Now, with no school to go to, he stayed home a lot, and I kept begging to go to my mother's restaurant, so finally he took me there for lunch. I loved the gleaming pistols hanging behind the rough wooden bar. The bartenders all wore cowboy hats, and the waitresses wore long, ruffled dresses, and the little cocktail napkins had cowboy riddles printed on them. I watched her whirling around the room, her slender legs peeking out from under the ruffled skirt of her cowgirl dress, her dark hair smooth and sleek under a kerchief, her cheeks pink. She looked beautiful. I couldn't understand why my mother hated her new job so much.

Walter and I ordered hamburgers. I had wanted steak because it wasn't something we never ate at home, but my mother leaned down and whispered, "Too expensive. Besides, it's disgusting." But it didn't smell disgusting when the people at the next table ordered it, and when my mother brought their steaks to them, she smiled and acted like they were special and the steak was delicious.

Walter smiled and said, "Hey, this is some hamburger sandwich." But he only ate a piece of it. I ate every drop of mine and all the lettuce and the parsley, and I was licking up the drops of ketchup from my plate with my finger when my mother came zipping by, frowned and scooped up my plate.

The remodeled rental house with the magic stairway had been rented to a family with twin boys my age. Unlike Steve back in Chicago, the Wilson twins treated me like an equal. We climbed trees together, sitting up in the branches talking about our favorite comic books and eating almonds, cracking the shells and throwing them through the leaves. They even named me Champion Tree Climber.

One night, I stayed later than usual to watch their new television set. A few of our neighbors had them by this time, but of course, my family was uninterested in these new frivolous toys. We sat on their living room floor watching a movie on the tiny screen about a beautiful dark haired woman who mourns her dead father. I didn't want to cry in front of the twins, but it wasn't easy when it got to the part where she remembered how much her father had loved her, how he had tucked her into bed and told her stories. I wondered if my father ever tucked me in or talked to me in the dark the way my mother did. The beautiful woman had long straight dark hair like I wished I had, full lips and pale skin.

When they came to the part where the dark haired woman is lying in bed crying over her poor dead father, I had to clench my jaw against my own tears. Suddenly, she's startled by a low sound. A shadow fell across her bed, and the beautiful woman pushed herself back against the pillow, her face filled with terror as she looked up toward the dark shadow spreading across the screen. "No, no," she screamed. It seemed so real, happening right in front of us in the living room. Even on the tiny screen, the people jumped right out into the room.

The story went on, and the young woman grew even paler and sadder as she went through her normal days in the pretty house where she lived with who? I wasn't quite sure if her mother was there with her or not. Then in the final scene, the young woman is asleep in her lacey bed full of pillows. I pictured it all pink and white like the kind of bed I wanted and was sure I'd never get because my mother thought that kind of thing too fluffy, too girly and too extravagant. The young woman's beautiful eyes were closed, and suddenly, there came that rustling sound. Her eyes flew open, her head turned toward the open window. "Father," she whispered in a sweet voice and her pale face lit with joy. But then, suddenly, she screamed, a horrifying scream that filled the tiny living room. It's not the good father, the one she longed for, who had come to visit her, but the one who had somehow turned into a devil bat. Recoiling in disgust, I wanted to turn to someone, to say: *But I thought he loved her. How could this happen? How did he get to be a bat when he was reading stories to her just a little while ago?*

I covered my eyes, but Tommy grabbed my arm and said, "Look, quick!" I watched in horror as she half raised herself up on one arm, her other hand pushing toward the ceiling, against something terrifying in the room with her. The rustling grew louder, and her body arced against what she saw coming toward her, hovering over her as she fell back, lying helpless in her bed. "No, no," she whispered, and the screen went dark. I could hardly breathe. I couldn't move. Even the twins had gone real quiet. Then Billy poked Tommy, and they started wrestling, and the spell was almost broken.

Later, when my mother came to get me, and we walked home together through the trees, I babbled on and on about the story. She seemed distracted, telling me when I paused for breath "it was just a movie." But then I told her how the dead father had turned into a bat. She looked at me, really saw me then, "You know," she said, smiling, "when we brought you home from the hospital, your father got up all night long to make sure you were breathing."

I hugged that father fact to me the rest of the way to our house. Surely that proved he had loved me. Yet, home in bed, every time I tried to close my eyes, I saw the beautiful woman's face, and I had to open them again. When Grandma came in to say good night, she bent down and whispered like she always did when she talked about my father, as if she were afraid he might be listening in another room. "When you father came home on leave from the army, he always went in to see you first before anyone else." After she left, I closed my eyes and pictured him bending over my bed, his cap pushed back, his uniform buttons shiny in the half light.

But when I finally got to sleep, I felt the room slip away, leaving me once again on the huge bed sheet that covered everything. This time as I started to run, I heard a kind of rustle behind me and when I looked down, I saw a shadow spread out on the sheet. The rustling grew louder, the giant wings reached toward me, and I woke up screaming for my mother.

My mother turned on the hall light and stood in the doorway. She looked cross. No smile for the silly movie in her eyes now. "How could a foolish movie scare you this much?" I didn't have an answer. It was just like those nights in Chicago when I had awakened her with the sheet ghost. Something about the tired slump of her body in her old bathrobe made me feel ashamed.

Over the next weeks, I kept seeing the beautiful woman's face over and over. Anything could set it off, scary music, shadows on the walls of my bedroom, the ringing telephone. Grandma came in sometimes when I called out and put the light on to drive away those huge wings that I could feel coming toward me in the dark. I tried the old dreams, tried riding the red horse to sleep, but something dark and evil waited for me. I could hear it breathing, droning like our old car engine. I knew if I kept my eyes closed a fraction of a second too long, I would see what the dark haired woman saw hovering in the air of her bedroom, and I couldn't let that happen.

My new public school, a few blocks down El Segundo Boulevard on the boundary between Compton and Inglewood was friendlier, more open, less threatening than my Chicago school had been. In the morning, the kids streamed into the low, ranch style building, one stream mostly white from the Compton side of the tracks and the other mostly brown from the other side. I started out in the second grade, but apparently, during the year I had stayed home before we left Chicago, I had pulled ahead reading at home, writing letters and learning arithmetic by keeping score when we played Crazy Eights. I finished the entire boring workbook the first few weeks of school. I thought it was better to get it over with quickly. Soon, they put me into third grade.

Shortly before school let out for the summer, I came home from school one day to find my grandmother crying into the dishwater. "Your poor mother's in the hospital," she told me, blowing her nose on a tissue.

I could feel my heart racing in my chest as I carefully set my books down on the counter. "What happened to her?"

"Nothing's happened--yet, little darling," she said. "She went to the hospital to try and save your baby sister or brother."

"But I don't have a baby sister or brother," I reminded her.

"You will," she said mysteriously as she put away the dishtowel and began to bang pots around which meant she was starting supper.

But during supper, they all kept reassuring me that *they* were only watching my mother overnight, and she'd be home the next day.

When Walter brought my mother home, she still had on the cowgirl dress she had worn to work the day before. He carried her into their bedroom and the adults fussed around settling her in bed. It wasn't until after supper that I remembered to ask her about the mysterious baby. I tiptoed into the bedroom. I thought she looked a lot like Sleeping Beauty lying there with her eyes closed, her hair dark against the white pillowcase, her skin luminous and pale. "Mama," I whispered. Her eyes opened, and she smiled, a pale smile. "Where's the baby?"

"Oh honey," she said, "the baby's still inside me, but I have to stay in bed from now on or else I might lose it." I already knew babies grew inside mothers, but I couldn't figure out how you could lose one so easily. It made me feel uneasy somehow, but I liked the idea of having a sister at last.

Later that evening when I went in to kiss her goodnight, I wrapped my arms tightly around her neck. I had thought of a new promise. Promises were sacred in our house. Once you said that magic word, you had to do it, no matter what. So it got saved for the really important things, like promising not to hurt someone's feelings.

"Ow," she said. "You're hurting me."

"Promise me," I told her.

"O.K. Let go. What is it?"

I let go of her neck. Instead, I took her face between my hands, so she'd have to look right at me when she said the words. "Promise me," I said, "That you won't die."

I saw her eyes grow darker. Her face grew soft under my fingers. She reached out and gently brushed my cheek with the back of her hand. "I promise," she said.

My mother made a lousy patient. Even Walter said so. All summer I breezed in and out of her room, secretly pleased at having her as a captive audience, even though she cried a lot.

"No one comes to see me except for you," she'd wail. "I could die right here for all anyone cares." Grandma suggested she take up crocheting, but my mother insisted she'd rather die than spend her time "tying stupid little knots."

One summer day when the sun shone hot enough to turn the small bedroom into an oven, we went out for a ride to cool off, leaving my mother behind, and when we got back, I stopped in to visit with her and found her wrapped inside Grandma's quilt.

"Aren't you hot?" I asked surprised to see her lying there so listless.

"I must have caught a chill," she said. Then Walter came into the room, and my mother looked up at him and said, "They called while you were out. They said they'd been waiting to hear from us, and we could save ourselves a lot of trouble if we'd cooperate. I told them only cowards bother a sick woman, and then I hung up on them." She closed her eyes.

Walter's quietly smiling face, the one he had brought into the house melted away in front of my eyes. "But who are *they*?" I asked.

Walter looked down at my mother as if waiting for her to answer, but she kept her eyes closed. He took a deep breath. "Some people in our government don't agree with what we believe in. They want us to give them the names of others who believe in the same things... the names of friends. They want us to tattle."

"But you're not bad," I said. "Just tell them about all the times you helped people. Like when the union helped people get more money."

"That's just it," said Walter. "That's the very thing they don't like."

My mother hadn't moved. I didn't like it; it was always a bad sign when people in my family got quiet. As long as they kept talking, they could keep anything at bay, but when they stopped, I knew trouble was close at hand. Silence, I had learned, was dangerous.

When my mother spoke again, she sounded tired, even more tired than when she came into my room at night to scare away the Devil Bat. "Those damn phone calls! I try to believe they're bluffing, but you don't know what to think. You pick up the paper, and it's full of red-baiting. Like the woman from Burbank who wrote into the paper to say she was 'desperately worried,' about the 'Communist infiltration.' What Communists? They're all either hiding or in jail." She looked up at Walter now. "And what about jobs? Teachers all over the country are losing their jobs."

"Maybe I should take my professor's advice and forget teaching, go into research and lie low for a while."

"Maybe we should all go back to the Midwest where we know people." said my mother. Then they got quiet and my mother blew her nose and looked at me and said, "Try not to worry, honey."

But how could I help but worry when it seemed we might leave California now that I had friends and liked my school? I wanted to do something to save us. But I had no idea what to do.

After that, when I woke in the middle of the night, I thought I heard the phone ringing. I tried to go back to sleep even though I knew I'd probably dream about the Devil Bat's daughter. During the day, the phone brought the ordinary voices of the Wilson twins, but at night while my friends slept snuggled safely in their beds, the ominous ring of the telephone mingled with the hum of wings and invaded my dreams. But I didn't ask who was calling any more.

By fall, it seemed like everyone at home got sick. Grandma came down with lumposy again like she used to back in Chicago. She hadn't had any attacks in California. She seemed too busy with the morning glories and the cats. But now, she took to her bed complaining of a sick headache. She cried off and on all day. "Where's Grandma?" I asked coming into the kitchen one morning to find my mother out of bed, wearing her sleep get-up of an old torn tee shirt and flannel pajama bottoms, spooning oatmeal into the bowls.

"Your grandmother's sick," she told me shortly, her face tight and cross looking.

"What's she got?" I asked. I was watching my grandfather trying to divide his oatmeal into neat triangles, but it kept sliding around in the dish, grey and sticky.

"Mocky's got the lumposy," he told me, not looking up. "A lot of old woman nonsense." My grandfather had finished dividing his oatmeal into triangles and was carefully eating it, one section at a time.

I wandered down the hall to my grandparent's bedroom and quietly opened the door. My grandmother lay in bed in the dark, her eyes closed, the blankets drawn up to her chin, like she used to do back in Chicago. She lay so still it scared me. "Grandma, are you awake?" I whispered.

She opened one eye. "Grandma's resting, little darling." Her voice had thinned, and her face looked pale without the rouge she usually wore. Something in her voice made me think she had been crying.

"Don't cry," I said like my mother always did.

She opened both eyes and smiled a very small smile. "This darn lumposy makes grandma awful blue."

"What is it? What *is* lumposy, grandma?"

Tears had started to ooze out from her eyelids and roll down her cheeks. "It's when," she said, "the world seems like such a sad place you don't think you can stand it. That's what lumposy is."

She was quiet a moment, then she said, "Your grandfather should have married a big, strong woman, not a weak thing like me." This was a sign that she had got caught up in the past, thinking about the baby boys. I never understood what triggered these forages back into the past, but I felt helpless to comfort her, and so I stood half in the doorway, leaning up against the jamb, loathe to come fully into the room and loathe to leave her. Then the door moved suddenly, and my grandfather brushed passed me. I watched him nervously, hoping he wouldn't tease her or shout at her like he sometimes did, and then they would go into their room and shut their door, and my mother would pull me down the hall and shake her head and mutter about them being "old fools." Now, he sat down on the bed and began taking off his shoes. "Why, daddy boy," my grandmother said, without opening her eyes.

He removed his shoes and carefully stretched out on the bed beside her. "Let's sing a tune for Mocky," he said, his only acknowledgement that I stood in the doorway watching. He began to sing his favorite, "John Brown's body lies a moldering in the grave..." He had closed his eyes too and folded his long, thick fingers across his chest. I watched them lying there in the dim bedroom, resting easy together, and I saw my grandmother take one of her tiny hands, the one wearing Aunt Bee's ruby ring and place it gently over her husband's gnarled fingers.

In September, I started fourth grade and was routed to a Mrs. Brown, a short, plump woman who reminded me vaguely of my grandmother. She stood in the doorway welcoming each of us with her brown eyes.

On the first day, she said, "In my classroom, there is only one crime I will not tolerate and that is the crime of looking down on someone because they are poor or because of the color of their skin." She cautioned us never to hold a grudge. "The most important thing is to forgive." That didn't sound like public school at all. In fact, it sounded a lot like the kinds of things we said at home, and I could feel myself relaxing into the seat.

Every morning she started the day in Spanish. "Buenos Dias," we would say all together. She had the Mexican-American kids in the class take charge of the morning ritual to teach us new Spanish words. While we stumbled over the unfamiliar sounds, the Spanish-speaking kids grew bolder and forgot to be shy. As the year progressed, these words grew familiar, becoming part of the classroom ritual, accepted into our lives.

She arranged our seats each week according to grades, and my new best friend, Fay and I took turns in the seat of honor, right next to Turtle Land, a special corner of the classroom where several boys kept their pet turtles and were allowed to race them on the playground at recess. We had the privilege of watching the turtles as they sunbathed on their mossy rocks, or paraded around their bowls.

Fay and I were sort of opposites, her with blond curls, me with dark, she plump and perky in flowered dresses, me, shy and skinny. But we were both smart. Several times a week, Mrs. Brown sent us to the blackboard to do what she called "mental arithmetic," a kind of rapid-fire math bee. She would call out a math problem while we stood with the chalk in our hands, poised over the board, and then quickly wrote the answers. Whoever wasn't fast enough or had the wrong answer had to sit down until there was only one student left at the board. Often that person would be either Fay or me. Although the class competed constantly, Mrs. Brown organized the class in ways that evened the odds for everyone, giving nearly everyone a chance to shine at what they did best. At home when I reported the day's activities, Walter thought Mrs. Brown ran her classroom creatively and fairly, traits I had learned in Chicago were hard to come by in the public schools.

The baby, who disappointed me by turning out to be a brother instead of the little sister I had wanted, was born in January, a month early. They named him after Grandpa, but everyone called him Burr because he made so much noise that Grandpa said he was like a little buzz saw. He cried day and night, doubling up his legs or stiffening his body and arching his back from some unseen agony. It didn't seem to me that anything that little could have so much feeling. My mother, still weak from months in bed, dragged herself around during the day.

Sometimes she cried along with the baby, pacing the floor with him in her arms, his body nearly upside down.

"Does he like that?" I asked one day, watching the baby bobbing in her arms, his head pointing toward the floor. It reminded me of the baby in Alice in Wonderland, the one who turned into a pig.

"God only knows," she said. "But I'd swing him from the treetops if I thought it'd relieve his pain and bring us all some peace.

"Is he ever going to do anything but cry?" I wanted to know.

"Of course. You did." That stopped me. I'd never thought of myself acting like this baby. It seemed like I'd always been too grown up to cry. "Just be glad you guys are not the poor Rosenberg children, orphaned in the name of *patriotism*." She kind of spit the last word like it left a bad taste.

I didn't get how we could go from a conversation about Burr to the Rosenbergs. But I was used to grownups who brought every conversation around to something from the past or some idea muddling around in their minds, seemingly unconnected to the day's events.

I knew about the Rosenbergs. In school, everyone talked about them as "dirty traitors who got what they deserved," while at home, my family went into a kind of mourning. I didn't join the other kids in the traitor talk, but I didn't exactly defend them either. It was like Chicago just more so. I was used to my family looking at an event in the news differently from everyone else. But these days I wasn't hiding in the corner of the playground. I belonged; better than that even, I had been best. Secretly, I felt badly for the Rosenberg boys too, but I didn't share any of that with my friends, and I tried to push it to the back of my mind.

"The Rosenberg trial has really brought the red baiters out of the woodwork," my mother went on. When I asked what "red baiters" were, she said, "They are people who call progressives names like "red" and try to blame the problems of the world on the very people who want to make the world a better place for everyone, not just for rich people." She paused a moment, then sighed and said quietly as if to herself, "impaled on their hysteria."

"What's impaled mean?" I asked.

That's how it went. You had to pick their statements apart word by word to understand them, and then sometimes I still didn't get it.

Grandma came in the room wiping her hands on her apron and answered, not very helpfully, "It means `done to death by slanderous tongues.'"

That didn't clear it up, so I tried again. "Are you going to jail?" I asked.

"Who said anything about jail?" My mother looked down at me, startled, like she just remembered I was there.

"Like the Rosenbergs."

"No one's going to jail," said Grandma.

"The whole country's lost their minds," said my mother. "The House Un-American Activities Committee seems intent on serving half the country subpoenas to appear before them. And then, if you answer their questions, you can be forced to name other people for them to harass, and if you plead the fifth, then you're considered guilty as charged and you're blacklisted and can't earn a living."

"Surely they can't black list everyone," said Grandma. "They're just making an example of famous people-movie stars and the like."

"Then how come all the teaching jobs seem to have dried up for Walter? Who knows what they'll do next?" said my mother, putting Burr over her shoulder and turning her face to the ceiling as if the answer might be floating up there somewhere

They started watching me more carefully. If I stopped with friends after school, I'd find my mother waiting on the stoop, a deep crease between her eyes. "Where have you been?" she'd yell, where everyone could hear her shrill voice.

Grandma tried to take some of the sting away by smiling at me with her eyes and saying, "Oh mistress mine where are you roaming?"

But it didn't help. I thought maybe because of the new baby she didn't love me as much anymore and at night when the Devil Bat woke me up, I'd lie in the dark and try to imagine what it would be like to be an orphan like the Rosenberg boys. Would they put me in an orphanage, a place I pictured like a jail for children where you would sleep on a pallet on the floor and eat gruel sort of like the oatmeal we ate but with none of Grandma's biscuits or oatmeal rolls for relief? I figured the Rosenberg boys and I would become friends like I was with the Wilson twins. But with them, I'd have someone to whisper with in the dark while we lay on our pallets, and they would understand what it was like to not belong anywhere because it seemed their family was even stranger than mine.

Sometime during those months, I thought I saw the gray car. I was walking down El Segundo Boulevard on my way home from school. The afternoon smog hung over the street like it often did, and a long gray car slithered out of the smog in the street beside me. It startled me, and I turned my head toward the car, and saw two men in the front seat. They stared at me for a moment, unsmiling, then sped up and drove away. I felt uneasy all the rest of the way home. But I decided not to tell my mother. I thought the men might be connected somehow to the Rosenbergs, and I didn't want to upset her even more.

One night during supper, my grandfather spooned the last pie wedge of mashed potatoes into his mouth and said, "Mocky and I are shuffling off to Buffalo."

"What does that mean?" I asked. I knew it didn't actually mean Buffalo. That's what he said sometimes when he left the house, but just the same, something in his voice seemed different. I could feel my stomach turn over.

"So," my mother said from the end of the table where she sat rocking the baby back and forth across her lap, "You're actually going to do it."

"At the rate this Cold War hysteria is escalating, we're liable to be at war with the Soviet Union any minute."

"That's nonsense," said my mother. "Even Harry Truman can't be that crazy."

"Los Angeles will be one of the first places hit," said Grandpa, calmly scraping up the last smidgen of potato.

My mother pushed back her chair, her eyes flashing. "How can you? To do this now? To sell this land just when it's going up in value is nuts, just plain stupid." She said it with conviction like she was thinking only about their finances and not about their abandonment. But I was feeling torn between not wanting to leave and suddenly worried about being "hit."

"Why don't you and Walter buy it then?" Grandpa asked.

"You know we don't have a pot to pee in right now." She hoisted the baby higher on her shoulder, got up and left the table. Walter went on picking at his food, but he looked sad, and Grandma was spooning up her food, not saying anything. When she caught me looking at her, she smiled, even though it wasn't her real smile. But I sat stunned. I had tried so hard to stay calm, to act like nothing bad was happening, and it seemed it hadn't helped at all.

A month later, the white house, the roses, and my mother's stairway to heaven sold to a lady realtor with a nose for a good deal. She even agreed to keep Molly. When I asked my grandmother why they decided to leave us like that, she said it was "high time they had a visit with Aunt Marjorie, and anyway now that your mama and new papa have a family, you don't need us anymore."

Here it was again: The new family had happened just like the new life without my permission, no matter how terrible I felt about it. No one had bothered to ask me if I wanted to trade this baby who cried all night and dribbled bananas for my grandparents. Once again, I felt our old life slipping away with only a shadowy ghost of a new one visible. Paradise had failed me after all.

But my mother acted like she didn't mind leaving. They had decided to head back to Chicago as soon as the school year ended. She said I should be happy; I was finally getting what I had wanted. But for me, everything had changed over the year. California had become a place where I belonged again, where for a while, we had seemed so normal. I couldn't understand how come I seemed to be the only one sad about leaving the almond trees or the roses. Even Grandma didn't talk to the morning glories any more, and my mother went around complaining all the time about California, about the smog, the traffic, the air. She said she couldn't breathe here. When I sulked, she said, "Thank God, we won't have to put up with this awful place much longer. I, for one, can't wait to get back to the Midwest where the sky's not full of smog all the damn time."

While my grandparents finished packing up the white house, we took a small apartment down the street in a square, cement four family building closer to school. My grandparents gave us most of the furniture, and my new bedroom was a whole lot bigger than my old one had been but the back door let out onto a concrete yard, and there was only one tiny window up near the ceiling. The day we moved, Annie hid out among the trees, and I had to drag her forcibly into the car. I didn't want the lady realtor to get everything I loved. But even though I made a nice bed for her in my new bedroom, she didn't seem to like the plain white walls and the cold linoleum floor any better than I did because she kept running away back to the old house. Every time I rode my bike down El Segundo Boulevard to bring her back, she'd stay a day or two, but then she'd be gone again.

When I complained to my mother, she said, "It's hard for her to give up the place she loves. Can't you love her enough to let her stay where she's happy?"

"But how come *I* can't stay there? How come *I* had to choose?"

"It's different for people," she said.

But I didn't see why, and I hated them all a little that spring.

The only good thing about moving was having Fay downstairs. I began to see another side of her, a side not apparent during school hours. Being the smartest kid in class, next to me, of course, Fay usually kept her sleek blond pony tail bent over her work. But at home Fay Jean's curls sprang free, and she lived and breathed romance. "Boy crazy already at nine years old!" my mother said and shook her head.

I saw it differently. It seemed to me Fay had a nose for adventure. Instead of the old cowboy games, she had discovered the thrill of chasing boys. She had a way of tossing her curls, and cocking her head to one side and giving a ready-for-anything look when we met in the afternoons in our secret hideout under the carport.

"Don't you think Junior looks a lot like Alan Ladd?" she asked me one day as we sat in my bedroom.

"Kinda." Junior was Fay's brother, older by a year. He wore a pale blond crew cut and bounded around the building in high top tennis shoes and raggedy blue jeans. Everyone in their family called him Junior and Fay, Sister. Secretly, I thought Junior was cute, but he didn't look much like Alan Ladd.

But Fay didn't really care that much about Junior's looks. Mostly, she wanted to talk about his friend, Bobby. "Don't you just love the cute way Bobby does his hair? It makes him look like Ronald Reagan in *Louisa*."

I tried to steer her away from Ronald Reagan, who she adored, because everyone in my family hated him. But my mother carrying clean clothes into my room had heard her and said, "Ronald Reagan's the world's biggest stool pigeon and a liar to boot." She threw the clothes onto my bed and went on about how Reagan went before some committee and told a lot of lies about people we knew, and now some of those people had lost their jobs or might even go to jail like the writer Dashiell Hammett because "*he* told the committee to stick it." She ended the lecture by saying, "So pick some other movie star to drool over," and flounced out of the room.

"Boy," said Fay, "your mother gets upset over the funniest things."

One day Fay brought Junior and his friend, Bobby over to our secret hideaway to play poker, a new, more sophisticated game. During our game, Bobby kept leaning over and giving Fay little pecks on the lips which embarrassed me and thrilled me at the same time. After we had lost all our chips to the boys who were gleefully scooping them up like they were rubies, Fay started talking in a bored sort of way about how movie stars hold their mouths together for a long time when they kiss. The conversation made me nervous, especially when Bobby and Junior started whispering together, looking over at us and laughing. Fay didn't seem to notice; she just went on looking up at the ceiling and humming to herself. Finally, Bobbie asked Fay to movie star kiss with him, and they pressed their lips together while Junior kept time with his watch. I grew more and more uncomfortable, and I thought they looked stupid sitting with their mouths crunched together while Bobby's face got red. Every now and then Junior looked up at me and smiled, and right then I knew he wanted to try it too.

After that day, Bobby and Fay would movie star kiss under the porch and if Junior wasn't around with his watch, Fay would punch out the time with her fingers. One night, just before dark, the doorbell rang, and it was Junior standing there by himself looking embarrassed. "Wanna walk around?" he asked.

I didn't really. I couldn't imagine what I'd talk to him about since we never spent five minutes without the others around, and Fay usually did the talking for all of us. But I felt sorry for him looking so uncomfortable standing there all sweaty, so I went outside. After about five minutes of walking around in silence, he said, "Well, I'd better go," and before I had a chance to even say goodbye, he had pushed his face down and put his mouth on mine. His lips felt dry and rough, and after a few seconds, I got impatient. I couldn't see what Fay saw in this. Finally, after what seemed like hours, Junior pulled his mouth away and held up his fingers saying triumphantly, "Ha! I punched out 60!" And he took the stairs two at a time back to their apartment.

When Fay heard, she was pleased with my progress. But my mother was not pleased. I found her in the bedroom, rocking Burr in her arms. She put a finger to her lips. But then she put him down in his basket, and I followed her out to the kitchen where she began the unending job of sterilizing baby bottles. I told her about the movie star kiss the way I told her about everything. I had learned that other mothers couldn't be trusted with kid stuff, but I had always been able to talk to mine about my friends. I looked for her the second I got in the house and told her every thought, every word. My mother laughed at my antics or just asked me questions, enjoying the story. Sometimes she turned the story into a lesson, but she rarely judged me or my friends. This time, she threw up her hands and said, "Good God, don't you kids have anything better to do?" That was the way she was these days, tense and distracted and at the same time, more easily irritated.

But if she had been cross over the movie star kiss, it was nothing compared to the pork and beans I had taken to hanging around Fay's house a lot, not because I felt exactly comfortable there, but more because they seemed exotic and I was curious. Fay's mother stayed home and cleaned house all day like my friend, Kay's had done back in Chicago. But while Kay's mother had always worn skirts and nicely pressed blouses as she went around their house and had baked a lot of chocolate chip cookies, Fay's mother wore shorts while she scrubbed the kitchen floor and always seemed to have a cigarette burning in the ashtray nearby. Fay's father never came home in the afternoon to take us swimming or anywhere else. He got home at 5:00 every day. His arrival usually announced to me by Fay, "Dad's home. Gotta go," and she'd take off at a run for their apartment upstairs.

One day, we had been looking at magazines in her tiny room that felt crowded with just a twin bed and a dresser. When Fay had seen my huge playroom for the first time she'd said, "Gee, I can't believe your parents gave you the *biggest* room."

"That's because I need some place to keep my toys. And besides, my mother says kids need privacy." Her eyes had grown big at that.

Now, when her mother announced the dinner hour, she said casually, over her shoulder that I could stay and eat if I wanted. A little thrill of excitement went through me. I had never actually seen her father up close, and I took this as a chance to get to know him a better. Real fathers were hard to come by in my world.

But almost immediately, I could see that I would learn very little. No one at the dinner table said much. Fay's father sat at one end of the dinner table and Fay's mother at the other. Junior sat across from Fay, and they squeezed a folding chair next to her for me. Fay's mother spooned beans out of a large pot at her end and passed the plates around the table. Then she passed around a plate stacked high with white bread. I had never eaten canned pork and beans before. It wasn't the kind of food my mother thought suitable for growing children, nor had I ever seen bread like this. We had Grandma's oatmeal bread or store bought wheat bread. My mother claimed white bread was just filler given to poor people. I took several slices of the downy bread, impressed by its color, pure white like cotton.

Fay's father sat with his crew cut bent over his food, silently spooning beans into his mouth, something grim and tired about his face. Walter didn't talk much either, but the silence at this table felt different, meaner somehow. He only spoke once during the meal. While I had quickly spooned beans into my mouth, fascinated by this new food, the new sweet flavor and followed Junior's lead by mopping up the juice with the bread pillows, Fay had mostly stared sullenly down at her plate. Suddenly, her father looked up from his plate, turned his head toward her and snarled, "You'd better eat those beans up quick, Sister, or you can sit here all night lookin' at them." Then he pushed his chair away from the table, got to his feet and left the room.

Fay's mother tightened her mouth. She looked down the table at Fay and shook her head. Junior just went on eating his beans, not looking at anyone. I don't remember how long we sat there or if Fay ever finished her food, I just remember sitting there bewildered by his anger, and at the same time, wondering why she didn't want her beans and wishing I could eat them for her.

When I got home that night, I couldn't wait to tell my mother about the new wonderful food I had discovered. But her eyes filled with disgust, looking at my face as if it might still be covered in sticky bean juice. "That's the kind of food you want--slop. Food that's fit for pigs not for children. My God, we'd better get out of here soon before you take leave of all your senses."

But still, she promised to let me go to church with Fay's family on Easter, and for a while, I felt almost happy again. I had never been inside a church. My mother said, "Religion's just an opiate for the masses." I didn't know exactly what that meant, but from her tone of voice, I could tell she was disgusted with it. Fay's family went to church every Sunday, and Fay had made Easter seem more like theater than church. She had talked about the lovely candles, the stained glass windows lit from behind by sunshine, the beautiful, sad music. I even got Grandma to promise me an Easter dress with ruffles. Fay already had a beautiful fairy dress made out of pale blue organza. When I went back to the other house, I saw Grandma had started cutting the pieces of my dress out of a peachy satin material, a little like my dress back in Chicago. I could imagine the rustle of the crinolines that would go underneath.

Then one day, my grandparents drove off in the old Lincoln they had bought for the trip to Colorado. We hadn't even known Grandpa could still drive, but in one of her characteristic moments of rapture toward her husband, Grandma had said, "Oh daddy-boy can do anything her puts his mind to!"

Grandma brought the pieces of the dress and turned them over to my mother.

"But you can't sew," I told my mother who gathered up the pile of dress pieces neatly pinned to sections of paper pattern.

"How hard can it be?" she shrugged. "Besides she's already done the hard part."

But I was worried. I knew my mother didn't approve of little girls wearing dresses. She believed in the sanctity of pants for one and all. Even back in Chicago, I had only had that one peach colored cotton dress, quite plain with some lace around the pockets, but a fairy tale dress to me. I used to pester her to let me wear it, but she usually said no, preferring to dress me in pants.

My mother took the dress pieces away into her bedroom and said, "Don't bother me about it. I'll finish the damn dress by Easter. Although why you want to go sit in some boring church with people who call their kids generic names is more than I can see."

Over the next couple of weeks, I couldn't help worry because I never actually noticed my mother working on the dress. Once when I went to check on it, I saw my mother had taken the same pieces out of the box, and laid them on the bed, but then she must have gotten tired because she had lain down next to them and gone to sleep. But I had to believe that somehow it would happen and gave Fay daily progress reports, making up details, whenever she bragged about her dress. At night I dreamed the dress floated around me like angel wings. In fact, I concentrated so hard on it that I barely thought about my grandparents who had left quietly and were now living in their new house in Denver.

On Easter Sunday, I waited in my room impatiently while my mother sequestered herself in the bedroom to put the finishing touches on the dress. Finally, at the last possible moment, she called me into her room. As I came down the hall in my slip, she stood in the doorway and mumbled around some pins still left in her mouth, "I had to pin some of it together. But it'll get you through church at least." I was trying to see it over her shoulder. She took the pins out of her mouth and smiled, a smile meant to be reassuring, but that didn't quite make it to her eyes. She had begun to have dark circles under her eyes all the time and today her eyes seemed darker than usual. "I had to make a few changes, "she said, "But it's so much more practical now." Then she stepped aside.

At first, I didn't see anything. I must have stared down at the bed for several seconds before I actually saw the grey skirt laid out ready for me to step into. I couldn't move, couldn't utter a sound. My mother must have felt my pain begin to seep into the air because her voice sounded less assured more hesitant, "Well, I know it's not quite what you wanted, but this skirt is more practical. Now you can wear it for other things..." But I wasn't listening. I felt something snap inside, let go in a flood of pure rage so intense that for a moment I couldn't even breathe, and then I began to scream. I stood there in front of the lumpy bed covered in its faded chenille spread, while torrents of sound fell into the room like shards of broken glass. I began to tear at the gray skirt.

At first my mother just stood there looking scared and stunned, but then she grabbed at my hands and slapped me. It worked like a drink of icy water, and the screams caught in my throat, stopping as suddenly as they had started. Now, I stood stunned into silence. Nobody had ever laid an angry hand on me before. Then she started pinning the grey skirt around me where it wasn't quite finished. She shoved the pins viciously through the cloth, while I stood as motionless as a stick, my arms and legs too heavy to move.

It was now too late to go with Fay's family, so she walked me over to the church herself. It was probably the longest walk we ever took together. We rarely went anywhere. My family didn't go in for aimless recreational activities. On the way she spoke once, "I don't know what's gotten into you." After that neither of us said a word. We walked, our only California walk together, through the smoggy Easter afternoon down El Segundo Boulevard, our eyes looking straight ahead, our arms not touching. Out of the corner of my eye, I saw a grey car slow down, then it moved ahead of us, then it slowed again. Almost too tired to care, I glanced over at my mother, but she stared straight ahead, seemingly indifferent

When we got to the church, she waited on the sidewalk while I went up the stairs. At the door, I turned and looked back in time to see her walking away, pulling her old blue sweater tightly around her. Something about the way she kind of hugged herself made a lump in my throat.

I spotted Fay right away, her head was turned half way around watching for me. She scooted over closer to Junior, and I squeezed into the pew. I had been worried I wouldn't know what to do in church, might somehow embarrass Fay, but I barely heard or saw anything that day. This had been my last chance to be a real California girl, frothy and pink like cotton candy instead of gray and sad. Instead, I sat in numb misery through the entire Easter service next to Fay in her pale finery, sitting very still in the gray skirt because every time I moved, one of the pins stuck me.

Soon after that Sunday, I decided to run away. I made the mistake of telling my mother about it at dinner. We were sitting at the makeshift table, a card table actually, and I said I was going to leave now. My mother passed me a plate of eggs and said, "Don't be silly. Where would you go?" She spoke to me like I was some adult friend deciding on an impractical vacation.

"Back to Chicago where we belong," I said, taking a huge portion of scrambled eggs.

My mother looked at my eggs and frowned. I knew she thought I had taken too much. She thought everyone could live on air and old union songs like she did. "Maybe you'll get your wish," she said. Then she changed the subject and I didn't say any more about it, but I kept thinking about it.

For a while now I had been imagining again that my father wasn't really dead, just missing, that he might walk through the door at any minute and scoop me up and say it had all been a mistake. I knew that the army didn't make mistakes like this very often, but I didn't care. This time it would be true, and the two of us would get on a train and go back to Chicago. He wouldn't let telephone calls scare him.

A couple of nights later, I was in my room reading when I looked up from my book and decided I couldn't stand it any longer: my mother tired and wrung out and Walter mostly silent and grim. I should just go. That would teach them. I could hear my mother putting Burr to sleep in the other room, her voice just barely coming through my closed door. Sometimes, she still sang the old bedtime songs. I got up and went over to the old dresser my grandparents had left behind after we moved out of their house. I remembered that my mother had stuffed a suitcase in the hall closet, and I opened the door and looked down the hall. She was still singing, and I could hear the creak of the rocker, so I tip toed down the hall and got it out and then carried it back to my room. I pulled everything out of my drawers and began making piles of pajamas, underwear, pants and shirts. I knew it was colder in Chicago, so I'd probably need a jacket even if it was nearly June. I got so absorbed in deciding what I should take and what I should leave behind that I didn't hear the door open and didn't notice my mother until she was standing nearly on top of me with a cup of tea in one hand. I saw her take in the piles of clothes, and she smiled down at me. She had that look on her face she got when she thought something I had done was cute. "Packing already?" she said. "I thought you didn't want to leave California." Something about her smile was making me really mad. I went on putting the neat piles of clothes into the suitcase, not looking at her.

"Maybe I'm not leaving California," I said, "just leaving you."

She went over to my bed and sat down, still holding the teacup. But I saw with satisfaction that the smile was gone. "Don't worry," I told her. "I have a plan. I've got the money I saved from my allowance."

"I see," she said, just sitting there, her face suddenly drawn again and tired.

But I couldn't let her off the hook, not so easily. We sat there for a few minutes while she sipped her tea, and I tried to think what to do next. Then it just burst out of me, "I would think that if your kid talks about running away twice in the same week, you should *do* something!"

"O honey," she said in a low voice, her old Chicago voice, her sad story voice. "We're working on a plan to get us all out of here. I wish there were something more I could do to make it better for you.

But for the life of me, I can't think of what it could be."

I sat, still squatting on the floor next to the half-packed suitcase, feeling the familiar mixture of sadness and anger. I didn't really want to leave them. I only wanted my life to be the same old life, when I had sat with Annie in the sun, waiting for my cousin Karen to visit, watching grandpa hoe the vegetables, then seeing him look up suddenly and grin at us and wipe the sweat from his face with his long, brown arm.

I remembered suddenly that I had never seen the ocean, not once in the nearly two years we'd been here. I thought of how Kay's dad had taken us to Lake Michigan in Chicago and how he'd tried to teach me to swim, how my mother had tried to lure me into wanting to leave Chicago by talking about the ocean, the waves, the surf, how I could become a good swimmer. But I hadn't become a good anything. I didn't even know what a surf was, and now, I'd never know. "I want to see the ocean," I told her.

She smiled at me then, the old understanding smile of our Chicago days. But we both knew it was too late to see the ocean.

During those last weeks in California, I fell into a kind of general misery that would become familiar to me over the years. My cousin Karen remembers kicking her feet against the bedroom floor and crying in frustration, but I remember no such outbursts during those final days in the golden sunshine. I remember more of a general feeling of malaise that slowed my steps, and even made me think slowly as if the very air I breathed poisoned me. I felt sick to my stomach in the morning Sometimes I'd start out for school, pushing through the smog which covered the tops of everything, turning the buildings into hazy dream houses, cutting off the tops of trees, hiding the sky, and I saw dim forms in front of me, boogiemen shapes, the sound of an engine slowing. I'd stare desperately into the smog, trying to penetrate the haze, but some days it seemed impossibly thick, and I'd have to turn back.

When I came home, slouching back into the house, I could see sympathy in my mother's eyes. She'd meet me at the door, carrying Burr, beaming at me from her arms. "Feeling sick again, honey?' she'd ask, smoothing back the curls covering my forehead. I'd nod miserably. Sometimes I'd give her a break by taking Burr and playing with him. At least, *he* was always glad to see me. But Easter Sunday had been my first inkling that nothing would ever make it right in California again, not my mother, not a new dress, not the friends I had tried to emulate

Fay still came over at night sometimes to tell me her amorous adventures, to toss her curls and make fun of Bobby's moist skin. "When he kisses me," she said, "he gets all warm and damp like a bath towel." But now she didn't always wait for me after school but went home with Laura instead. I told myself it didn't matter; it was only natural she would find a new friend to take my place, one who would stick around a while. Her abandonment just melted into the general misery of those final months in California.

In Mrs. Brown's class, I felt weightless, everything once firmly in my grasp, now slid through my fingers. Laura used to be way behind us on the blackboard where Mrs. Brown kept our scores from a mental arithmetic game we played each morning. She even arranged the seats according to who had the highest score. Now, it was Laura and Fay who vied for first place. I watched my name on the blackboard slip from first to third and finally one awful day to last place. I sat at my desk and stared at my name firmly written at the bottom. All day my eyes kept turning toward it, drawn irresistibly as if a message flashed across the room. *Christine Is Last.* Even the pale boy's name was ahead of mine. He had improved, while I had fallen.

Just before school ended, we held the Grand Turtle Race right after lunch. On a beautiful warm day when the smog had cleared and the sky was blue, and we all trooped out to the playground, excited by being outside when the rest of the school sat trapped at their desks. The boys drew a kind of racetrack onto the pavement with fresh chalk while we stood round shuffling our feet and talking in excited whispers. Then the boys placed their turtles on the start line, Mrs. Brown gave the signal, and they were off. But the turtles seemed to have missed the significance of the day, and they ambled along, often meandering outside the designated race lines. The boys had to reach down and scoop them back inside.

Before long, the two turtles everyone seemed to be watching belonged to Robert, a popular boy and the only black boy in the class and the pale, dirty white boy everyone picked on. Everyone kept cheering for Robert's turtle, slower and more lackadaisical. Clearly Robert was the preferred winner. Pretty soon the kids began to get bored and to wander off into little clusters. But I stayed, squatted down beside the track. Robert, bending over in front of me, frowned in concentration as he whispered encouragement to his turtle who lagged far behind, even jiggling a stick to prod him on. On my other side, the pale boy acted bored. His eyes roamed around the playground, and he smiled his lazy smile at no one.

As the turtles meandered toward the finish line, someone fell and distracted everyone's attention. Even Mrs. Brown moved away from the turtles and went toward the noise. A sudden movement to my side made me turn my head back toward the race track, and in that instant, I saw the pale boy scoop up Robert's turtle from outside the track and place it well ahead of his own. It happened so fast I couldn't be sure I had really seen it, and I turned toward the pale boy who kept staring down at the ground.

Then Robert shouted in glee because he had won, and Mrs. Brown congratulated him, and the other kids crowded around to cheer the champion, the turtle everyone loved, the one they had been afraid would lose. Neither the pale boy nor I had moved. Then he turned his head suddenly and our eyes met. The smile was gone, and I saw in his eyes that he knew I had seen. I smiled right at him. I tried to smile *I'm sorry I hated you for smelling bad, sorry you're always alone, that we didn't want to play with you* and suddenly without warning, I felt tears in my own eyes. He looked away, reached down and scooped up his turtle.

"Just a dumb ol' turtle race," he whispered.

Much later my mother would tell me that she had read in the newspapers about a woman in California who was accused of being a Communist and had her child taken away from her. But back then, I had no idea what could be making her so constantly angry. I thought it must be something I had done to make her eyes glare at me with such hatred. I'd stand there sullen on the yellow brick path with California flowering sweetly around and wonder what had happened to that pretty woman who had pretended to be a tree bending in the wind, who had sung Paul Robeson songs or danced in long, bright ruffled dresses? But most of all, I wanted her to see that I was just like the pale boy nobody liked, that the sunshine in California had disappeared into the smoggy air, and I thought it had to do with me. Maybe I was somehow dirty or hateful or unacceptable. I wanted her to really see me standing there curly haired and sullen, something un-American about me now.

I remember nothing about the actual packing up or getting ready for a long trip. Later, I would tell people I hated California, the place where I had learned to climb trees and hang out with boys, where I had stood at a blackboard performing feats of magic arithmetic, feeling quick and smart and beyond harm. Unlike the journey from Chicago, leaving California is missing completely as if my body levitated over the fruit trees, up and away from the apartment building without my conscious mind cooperating at all. I passed through the smog, dead to sound and sight, and it would be fifty years before I could bring myself to return there.

One day sitting in class in the middle of a quiet study time, everything cleared for a moment, like a veil lifting. Mrs. Brown sat at her desk grading papers, my classmates bent over their work. I sat, taking slow, deep breaths, imprinting them on my mind. Alert to any disturbance in the field, Fay looked up. Our eyes met and she smiled, a thoughtful smile, like something about my face had caught her off guard. For a moment, I could almost believe nothing had changed. At the end of the day, she would be waiting by the side door, and we would saunter down El Segundo Boulevard in the sticky sun, pomegranates hanging ripe for the taking. With all the time in the universe, we would link arms and skip in time to the day. But then Fay returned to her book, leaving me alone with my shame, knowing I had failed to live up to her expectations, believing that if she knew the real truth about me, knew about the gray car, or the phone calls, she would hate me even more. She would know I had never been the person she thought I was with a normal family who ate pork and beans together and had a real father to yell at them like Fay's did.

The grown-ups in my family were suspected of terrible things, and I knew in my deepest heart that they could not be guilty of anything truly bad. I had watched how they treated our neighbors, how much most people liked them. I knew they were the kind of people Mrs. Brown would like if she could only know them as they really were, not like comic book caricatures of red demons.

Most of all, I wanted to take away the disappointment in Mrs. Brown's eyes the day I gave her the note from my mother explaining about the bad stomach and asking if I could come late to school. I wanted to give her back the real me, the one who had climbed trees and won blackboard races, but she alluded me, lost somewhere in a smoggy California morning. That day Mrs. Brown had looked at me for a minute, trying to read my face with her kind eyes. Then she said softly, "Tell your mother it's alright for you to come late if it's necessary, but I don't really understand."

I stood there in front of her desk, my eyes watching the little gold pin she wore on her dress, and I wanted desperately to explain it to her. But even if I had trusted her enough to tell her about the midnight phone calls, or the strange car, I didn't have the words. I was nine years old, and there was so much to say and no words to say it in.

I dream that I am walking home from school again down El Segundo Blvd. The sun is shining on the pomegranate trees along the street, and the street is quiet, still, like a movie set. The trees, the lawns, even the sun in place as it should be, as it is every day when I walk this same block to the little white house set back from the street, framed by morning glories and roses. I turn onto the yellow brick walkway, and now my steps quicken as I hurry to the front door, anxious to be home, to have out my heart to the ones waiting just beyond the door to hear all that I have seen and heard during the long school day. I run up the steps, pull on the screen door, but it is locked. Puzzled, I ring the bell. The door opens almost immediately, and our neighbor Mrs. Smith is standing in the doorway on the other side. Why is she there? Why is she frowning at me through the screen? "Hello, Mrs. Smith," I say. Where is my mother?"

But she continues to stand there frowning. Then she says in a flat voice, the voice of a stranger, "I'm sorry, but I don't know who you are." And she shuts the door.

I stand there on the front steps silenced. She does not come back, and I know deep in the pit of my stomach that my family has gone somewhere I cannot follow, disappeared somewhere in the smoggy afternoon.

...And what about the children? This was a topic of earnest conversation. Suppose both parents were clapped into jail, what happens to young children? People worried about it. They made private arrangements with kin or friends, who were thought to be less vulnerable. Perhaps the questions about children seemed so real, so urgent, convey in personal terms the political ambience in those June and July days of 1951.

    -Al Richmond, *A Long View from the Left*

In 1951, he [Dashiell Hammett] went to jail because he and two other trustees of the bail bond fund for the Civil Rights Congress refused to reveal the names of the contributors to the fund. The truth was that Hammett had never been in the office of the Committee and did not know the name of a single contributor.

The night before he was to appear in court I said, "Why don't you say that you don't know the names?"

"No," he said, "I can't say that... I hate this damn kind of talk. But maybe I better tell you that if it were more than jail, if it were my life, I would give it for what I think democracy is and I don't let cops or judges tell me what I think democracy is." Then he went home to bed, and the next day he went to jail.

    -Lillian Hellman, Introduction. *The Big Knockover* by Dashiell Hammett

The mood is 1952 was much grimmer than in 1947. It was easy to laugh at the Committee during

its first go at Hollywood; the hearing room had a circus atmosphere. It was still the old Dies Committee then, the government's scruffy black sheep. But in 1952 the committee that had sent Alger Hiss to jail would vault Richard Nixon to the vice-presidency. Even McCarthy's committee in the higher chamber drew much of its menace from the record of the House Committee. Yet the pickings were slim for Communist-hunters. There were no more Hiss or Rosenberg cases to be found. The State Department had been purged and purged. The old lists were getting shopworn. Evidence was hard to come by. For lack of other fuel, the fire was eating into the constitutional framework itself. The charges became wilder—General Marshall was disloyal. Crazily, McCarthy's very lack of results fed suspicion—the government was successfully covering up, the Communists were going uncaught...

-Gary Wills. Introduction. *Scoundrel Time* by Lillian Hellman

DENVER 1952

When we stopped in front of Aunt Marjorie's house, my nose caught the odor of horse manure. Instead of my grandparents standing in the yard waiting for us, I saw real horses prancing about in a real corral across the road from the tall house sitting up on a hill. Aunt Marjorie turned off the car engine and said in her deep voice, "I don't know what those two old fools are thinking--going off to farm in the Ozarks at their age!"

My heart skittered. The name "Ozarks" sounded foreign. I couldn't imagine where my grandparents had gone. As usual, I skirted the subject, hoping somehow to avoid the hard truth. "What are Ozarks?" I asked Aunt Marjorie.

But no one answered. My aunt turned her head to look down at me, wedged between them in the front seat, and over at my mother. Strands of hair had escaped her tight bun, brushing against her cheek in wisps, canceling her plain jacket, her sensible shoes, making her face tender. She patted my cheek. Then she looked across me at my mother and said, "They want to have their cake and eat it too. Dad won't give up thinking he's head of the family. Well, I tried, but it didn't work out for us to live together." My mother nodded as if she understood.

All I knew was the one thing that had kept me going these past weeks was the idea of seeing my grandmother, of being able to follow her around the kitchen again, of getting something to eat besides broiled chicken and scrambled eggs. But even though I felt something burning in my chest, I tried to focus on the horses. "Can I ride one?" I asked my aunt.

"Uncle Richard knows all about that," Aunt Marjorie told me with a smile. Then we got out of the car, everyone talking at once, and Uncle Richard, a large, red faced man, came out for the suitcases, and we filed into the house. I walked behind my mother, who carried Burr asleep on her shoulder, craning my neck, listening for sounds from the corral. My grandparents got packed away with my father in a back corner of my mind--one of those things I would have to figure out for myself.

Later, my mother sat at the dining room table, going through a pile of mail that had been waiting for us, her head bent over her tea cup, her face more relaxed than I had seen it for a while. As she sorted, she made little sounds of surprise and pleasure. "Look, honey." she waved envelopes at me, "Letters from Kay."

"Why'd she send them here?" After we first got to California, I had written Kay several letters, but she never answered. When I went to my mother with my disappointment, she had said, "It's not that she doesn't still like you, but people have to get on with their lives." But if she really did like me, I had thought, she would answer. She would tell me she missed me.

Now my mother and Aunt Marjorie exchanged a look. "This is the address I gave them," she said simply, and handed me several envelopes with Kay's large, scrawling handwriting on the outside. If she had been given the Denver address instead, I had suffered over her betrayal for nothing. I opened the letters. I could tell right away that she never got my letters either She was wondering why I hadn't written to her. "There," my mother said, "and you were worried. See? It was all a big misunderstanding."

But I still didn't understand how all those letters could have gone astray. I thought I had given them to Walter to mail, leaving them in a pile on the kitchen table for him like we always did because my mother just wasn't any good at mailing things. "Somehow, I can't seem to get the letters into the box," she would say.

My mother looked over at my aunt. "Not that this did any good--they found us anyway." She came down hard on the "they," and my aunt nodded, her face serious. But when she looked over at me, she smiled in a way I knew was supposed to be reassuring. Suddenly, I knew this was about politics again. I felt it in my body, the way my stomach clenched up like it did whenever I had seen the gray car driving slowly down El Segundo Boulevard. We sat in silence while we read our mail. Then my mother looked up over the letter she was folding and said it was time for bed.

"But we haven't had supper yet," I said.

"You had cereal in the car earlier." She looked over at Aunt Marjorie. "All this child thinks about is food. Like her father." The cereal had been a new bran kind, and I had eaten it dry, right out of the box.

But Aunt Marjorie smiled and winked at me. "Your father used to eat half a beef roast at a sitting. I thought he and your mother would eat us out of house and home when they were dating. I think there's some pot roast in the ice box right now." And she went off to get it while I sat quietly turning this over in my mind--the idea of my father and mother eating real food together at some long ago dinner table. I pictured them putting butter on their potatoes, eating chunks of roast beef on matching white plates, calm and orderly and quiet.

After I ate the pot roast and some tiny carrots and miniature potatoes with their red skins still on and real butter melted over them, I still wasn't a bit tired, so Aunt Marjorie pulled me onto her lap. We sat in a rocker next to the dining room table where my mother sat playing with her tea bag and rubbing her hair back from her face. I thought she was the one who looked like she should be in bed.

My aunt rocked me while my long legs dangled awkwardly over her lap. "I rocked your mother," she told me, "back on Cook's Place, just like this." Then in a voice nearly as deep as Grandpa's, she sang to me: "John Brown's body lies a moldering in the grave, while the truth goes marching on."

It wasn't quite like having Grandpa sing it, but it made my mother cry. "When Walter gets here with our stuff," she said, blowing her nose, "we're going back to the Midwest, back home." Back, I thought, to our real life.

My mother began to tell Aunt Marjorie about the past year, about the phone calls, about the smog, how California had failed us. She told her about the friend who had come to visit while she was still in bed waiting for Burr to be born. "I was desperate for someone to talk to. I told her about the phone calls asking us to come down to headquarters and tell them about people we knew. My friend's eyes looked puzzled, then pitying. When I stopped for breath, she said I should try to get more rest, and then she left soon afterwards. She didn't believe me! She thought I was sick and imagining things, or worse, that I was just plain nuts! After all, how could this *democratic country*," and she bit the words off in disgust, "be guilty of calling up and harassing a sick woman? That's when I realized how alone we were." It came pouring out of her, the fear, the tension of waiting for the next phone call.

I sat on my aunt's lap surprised to learn that she had felt alone just like I had those last weeks in California. But after a while, I stopped listening and their voices became background music that mixed with the squeak of the rocker, rhythmic as a heartbeat.

A couple of nights later, the phone rang during supper and Aunt Marjorie answered it in the kitchen where we were eating meat loaf and mashed potatoes. My aunt was big on nutrition too, putting oatmeal and tiny chunks of green pepper into her meat loaf. But somehow she still managed to cook real food. I was savoring my meal, loving the meaty taste, the pepper chunks. But when the phone rang, I stopped eating. She handed the phone to my mother with an odd look on her face.

"Hello," my mother said, then, "Oh dear." Then, "Oh." My heart started to pound. Phone calls were never good omens in our family. When she hung up, she turned to the rest of us sitting at the table, waiting. "That was some guy who owns a filling station out in the desert. He said that our car broke down, and Walter took the bus.'"

"The bus!" exclaimed Aunt Marjorie, "where's all your stuff?"

I had stopped eating during the phone call. I realized that all of my dolls packed away in that trailer were now sleeping in some greasy filling station.

"Apparently," said my mother, "Walter and this man made some sort of deal, and the man promised to send everything here."

But when Walter finally arrived a few days later, he looked like the heat had gotten to him. Three days on a bus left him unshaven and haggard. He looked, my mother said, "like the wreck of the Hesperus."

With all of our worldly goods still out there on the desert, they were loathe to move on, even though I reminded them that everything would be fine once we got back to our old life. Then they reminded me that our old life had changed since we wouldn't be living in our old apartment, and Grandma and Grandpa had taken off for the Ozarks. They decided to stay put and earn some money. They both went out and got jobs, leaving Burr and me to blend in with my aunt's family. But we didn't blend so well.

They moved things around, making room for us in what was not a big house. My aunt and uncle and cousins slept upstairs, and they gave me the only other upstairs bedroom, which was more like a hallway since it was the only route to the bathroom. Walter and my mother and Burr made a place downstairs on a large enclosed back porch.

My mother and Aunt Marjorie sat at the kitchen table, sometimes all day, drinking tea, smoking cigarettes and making fun of the way the "Denverites" walked around downtown in cowboy hats and boots, calling them "coo-boys," while my older cousin Christie, a brown haired sixteen year old goddess, sat around reading movie magazines and drinking cokes. Kiely, the younger cousin, followed me around, demanding everyone's attention. She reminded me of an angrier, curly haired version of my cousin Patsy. Burr spent his time toddling in and out of the smoky haze in a cowboy hat and tiny boots, carrying his doll upside down by one foot screaming, "Hotfire," his only intelligible word, over and over and getting into things. But I only had eyes for the horses.

I spent a lot of time hanging around the barn hoping my uncle would let me ride. "Stay out of the barn," he cautioned me. He acted nervous around me, like I might break something. But I couldn't stay away. All those days spent playing horse in my backyard in Chicago, or dreaming about running off on Trigger with Kay along-side me on Champion, kept me glued to the corral watching the horses stand around whisking flies off their backs with their tails like beautiful golden brooms. I loved every inch of them, loved the way they came in colors, from a reddish-brown the color of rust to a soft golden brown like root beer candy barrels, and a dusky gray like old fence posts. I loved their manes that stretched long and full like Aunt Marjorie's hair when she took out her bun at night and her thick dark hair fell over her shoulders, unchanged, I imagined, from when they had all been young together back in their days on Cook's Place. I loved watching the horses take little, prancing steps toward me when I brought them carrots, so they'd let me touch their soft noses. I even loved the way they turned their smooth rumps and casually dropped their turds into nice neat piles wherever they felt like it, then walked away, tossing their heads in a frisky way that reminded me somehow of Fay.

When Uncle Richard let me sit on the golden brown horse they called Prince, and I looked down, the ground seemed very far away. Then Prince snorted, turned his head and pulled back his lips. His yellow teeth protruded from his huge lips like Halloween teeth in a grin, or maybe a growl in horse language. Instead of holding my head back and looping the reins over the saddle horn, the way I'd seen my cousins do, I slouched forward, gripping the saddle horn and holding on for dear life.

"She had that horn in a death grip," my Uncle said later with a laugh.

When I thought my Uncle wasn't listening, I whispered to Prince, trying to let him know I liked him, but I couldn't tell if he liked me back or not.

I asked my mother why Uncle Richard wouldn't teach me to ride, and my mother said quickly that Uncle Richard was too busy. He worked long hours running a drugstore, and I should leave him be. So I went back to hanging over the fence watching my uncle lead my little cousin around the corral while she sat on Prince, who strutted around and swished his lovely golden tail.

One day, I decided that if I couldn't ride the real horses, I'd become a horse. I began galloping around their yard, making horse noises, and sometimes refusing to answer when anyone called me Christine, pretending my real name was Trigger or Prince. No one paid much attention. My aunt or my mother would come out to the yard where I was galloping and say, "It's time for lunch, Prince." When I went downtown with my mother, I got books from the library on horses, and learned the different breeds. I started keeping complicated genealogies of imaginary horse families in a spiral notebook tucked into a pant pocket and carried with me everywhere.

That summer I learned to swear. Our family didn't really approve of swearing. It's not that they felt there was anything morally wrong with it, but as Grandpa put it, "a person shows his limited vocabulary by swearing." They felt themselves above using such words. One day when my cousin and I fought, and Uncle Richard yelled at me, and my mother said, "Try to get along--this is their house, after all," I squinted my eyes and said, "Who gives a shit?" and enjoyed the surprise on her face.

By late summer, the tension hung in the crowded house like a thick fog. Walter and my mother went out house-hunting, and finally found us one of our own, across town where the Mexicans lived. It sat back from the street all by itself, surrounded on all sides by a sea of mud. Covered in red tarpaper, sitting on a cement slab poured over the ground, it resembled a train car, derailed and stalled in the dirt.

The day we moved in, late in August, just before school started, the landlord, a stocky, baldheaded man who lived on the other side of the field, came out onto his porch and narrowed his eyes and watched the parade struggling across the mud with our belongings. Walter and Uncle Dick carried our few pieces of donated furniture: a rocking chair, two small dressers, two beds, an old wooden crib, and a kitchen table with three chairs painted a brownish-green color my mother said reminded her of vomit. My cousin Christie and I carried some paper bags with our clothes, and Kiely held onto Burr, who kept trying to dart out into the mud.

After we got our things sort of in place, we all went out to squeeze together on the tiny porch and stare out into the fields. My mother said she felt like the Joads in *The Grapes of Wrath.* She looked sadly at the cement foundation and said, "No matter how poor we were back in Michigan, we always had a cellar."Later, after my aunt's family had left and we finished putting our odds and ends of dishes away, I remembered my dolls, lost somewhere in the desert. "Do you think the man who bought the car will at least send my dolls?" I asked my mother. She was putting Burr to bed in his crib in the middle of what was supposed to be the living room. We didn't have any living room furniture anyway, except for the old rocker my Aunt donated, so the crib kept it from looking so empty.

"I don't think so," she said, bending over to tuck in Burr's blanket.

"Maybe he'll see them and remember," I persisted.

My mother straightened. "No, he won't," she said "because they're not there. We left them in your uncle's garage in California."

I struggled to take this in. "Left them? In California?"

My mother's forehead began to crease up like it did when she got cross. "Oh for heaven's sake, there wasn't room for everything. Stop worrying. Just be glad they're safe in the garage and not out there on the desert somewhere."

"But Molly-the-leper-doll needs someone to take care of her," I told her.

"We'll send for them when we've time and money. In the meantime, play with something else. Read books."

I could hardly believe they had left them behind, not even bothered to tuck them in beside the old chairs, or inside the bag of my mother's drapery material, all stuffed into the trailer. My mother shoved the covers under the crib mattress with sharp thrusts, her eyes like enemies.

I looked around the bare living room, gazing flatly at the un-curtained windows, and tried to brace myself against the enormity of this betrayal. My eyes were drawn to the wooden rocking chair, bare and lonely in the corner. This place, I thought, did not want to rock children to sleep, did not have stories to tell them. Suddenly, the air shimmered in the room, became thick, so that it caught in the back of my throat when I tried to breathe it. As I went toward my bedroom, I heard my mother call out, "Hey, do you want to come into the kitchen and talk to me while I make supper?" More eggs, I thought. I kept moving toward my room. The air had grown so dense it was like moving through swampland. Lucky for Burr, I thought as I passed him peacefully sucking on his doll's foot, lucky for him he was only a baby.

Walter got a job in a factory working third shift, and my mother worked in the early evenings as a waitress in the airport's restaurant. On my mother's waitress nights, Walter and I mostly listened to the radio. We'd turn on Fibber McGee and Molly while she put on her black and white uniform with the cute little black bow tie, then rush out the door, always late and angry about it, just like when she had worked at the cowboy restaurant in California. Again, I thought it sounded like fun.

One morning, I'd made the mistake of trying to cheer her up while she drooped around the kitchen in her bathrobe. "It must be neat to work at an airport."

"Neat?" Her voice had a frosty edge.

"I mean you like planes and all."

"I wanted to *fly* planes, not watch them out of the window while I feed steaks to fat businessmen." Then she slammed the pan of scrambled eggs on the table and left the room. I sat there looking at the eggs all crusted to the sides of the pan, and I wondered if maybe they let *her* eat steak too. I wanted to ask if she got to eat french-fries sometimes, but I didn't dare. I pushed away the frying pan, feeling like my throat was already stuffed with eggs, wanting to be back in the California nut trees. Already those last painful California days had retreated in my memory, leaving only the scent of blossoms. I wanted to be back in the doll hospital in Chicago, anywhere but here. And I wondered what had happened to the mother I had loved, the one who used to sing union songs and dance like a tree? I would rather have her jumping around the living room, no matter how silly she looked, than stalking around the house with her face thin and tight. Burr toddled in, and I picked him up and hugged him, feeling sorry for him suddenly because he had only a ghost for a mother. He'd never know the beautiful movie star woman she once had been.

Sometimes there was a gap between the time Walter left for work at night, and the time she came home, and Burr and I were alone together.

They figured since I was almost eleven, I was old enough to be alone that short while. But I was scared. I began to spend hours every night lying awake, listening for the sound of Walter shutting the front door, and until I heard my mother open it, I'd lie and think about my real father, wishing he would come to rescue me. Maybe we'd take Burr too. I hummed the song Grandpa used to sing to me back in Chicago about the strawberry roan. And I cried secretly, scrunching down inside the covers like I had in Chicago, but even more ashamed now, knowing I was too old to cry, and if my mother heard me, she'd say, "Don't be a calf. Only babies cry."

Every night, way into the winter, after it had started snowing, and the wind rattled the windows, I cried myself to sleep. I actually looked forward to the end of the day when I could go into my room, shut the door and cry. When I finally slept, I dreamed of creatures that slithered over the sheets, staring at me with glittering eyes like terrible fish seizing the bedclothes with their long teeth, pointed on the ends like knives.

As the days grew shorter, the neighborhood kids gathered in our mud lot among the broken bottles and cans to play Korea. My parents called the Korean War a "blot on history." They said we were interfering in the affairs of another country. They said the Korean people were having a kind of family argument that was none of our business.

I didn't care. The shouts of the kids outside had caught my attention. I raised my head and felt the air stir. When I put down my book and ventured to the back door, I saw swarms of kids waving their arms and running like wild horses through the cans and broken bottles out in the mud lot. Gradually I was drawn in, accepted without question, just another dark haired kid in the Mexican-American neighborhood. I ignored it when my playmates shouted, "Kill the Commies." If my friends wanted to kill imaginary North Koreans, I could shrug it off, and without qualms, I threw myself into the game.

The game had simple rules: We pretended to be American soldiers, and the cars going by on the road were all North Koreans. We'd start on one end of the mud field in small clusters, then crouch and run across the lot toward a large pit in the middle that we used as our foxhole. As we ran, we shot at the cars. If a car went by and caught you in its headlights before you made it to the hole, then you were killed and had to go to the end of the line and start over again. I loved the running, the excitement of dodging the headlights. For the first time since we left California, I was back outside, and a lot of the time I'd be ahead of the other kids. If I saw a car coming, I would take a flying leap and dive right into the big hole, not even caring if I scraped an arm or bruised a knee.

One night, just as we started across the lot, together in a low crouch, and headed toward the lights of an oncoming car, I saw our screen door open out of the corner of my eye, and my mother stepped out onto the cement stoop. My heart stopped. I could just see her making some dumb speech about how Korean problems were none of our business, or worse, she might even say she hoped the Communists won, that it would serve the U.S. right if they got kicked out of there. She talked like that sometimes, as if the United States were some foreign place, one she didn't much like. If she started in, I knew I'd die right then and there. Crouching in the mud, I peered through the dusty night. My mother stood there hugging herself against the cold, watching. Then a kid yelled, "Charge!" and we started running toward our foxhole. As I jumped, I heard the screen door bang shut, and when I turned toward our house again, I could see the empty stoop illuminated clearly in the pale moonlight, but beyond the screen door, I saw only darkness.

Wanda, my new best friend, played Korean war games with me. She had a round, pale face and lank brown hair that usually looked a bit snarled, like she never combed it. Something about her sad eyes made me feel a kind of kinship with her, and at the same time, made me want to be mean to her. Sometimes she'd be stumbling along, hesitating, slow as mud, and I had to push her into the hole, so she wouldn't get shot. When I made her cry, it made me feel braver. But then I'd feel guilty because I liked her. I liked her partly because her family's house looked as bad as ours.

They rented from a man who lived out of town and didn't seem to mind that the house hadn't seen any paint for about a hundred years and none of the windows opened. Wanda's mother said "It don't matter nohow because the cracks let in enough air to freeze a body anyway." They talked differently than anyone I had ever known. My mother said they talked like people who hadn't had much education. But I liked the way they sat around just like we did, talking in stories.

One day, sitting in the crowded living room cutting out paper dolls with Wanda, half listening to the adults, my ears picked up the word "Chicago." At our house it was mostly the women who sat around the kitchen table, but at her house they all crowded into the tiny living room. Since her father usually got laid off from somewhere every week or so, he was usually sitting on the sofa right where the sagging springs made a hump, usually with a Coors beer in his hand. That was another thing my mother didn't like about them. She said if he was going to drink himself to death, why didn't he pick a beer company that wasn't owned by "fascists"? Mr. Thomas didn't seem to care about that. No one paid any attention to that kind of stuff at Wanda's house; they didn't even mind the dog hair that covered every surface, so that when I played there, it stuck to my clothes. When I got home, my mother made me stand outside even if was dark out, to brush off every last hair before she'd let me in.

Mr. Thomas said, "Them big cities are just full of sin. Folks livin' in the underground tunnels where the streetcars go, livin' like rats in a sewer."

I couldn't believe they were talking about Chicago like that. I cleared my throat, "My mother says "underground" is a symbol. It isn't a real place." I remembered the night soon after we came to Denver when she told me a lot of people were living "underground," meaning hiding out. Then she sat down on my bed, and her eyes got serious, the way they did when she explained "important things." "Remember your lost letters to Kay? We had all of our mail sent here to Denver because those men who used to call us in California want Walter and me to tell them things about our friends, things we believe are none of their business, and so we are trying to keep them from finding us and bothering us anymore."

"Why don't we go back to Chicago? We'll be safe there."

She had brushed my hair back from my face and sighed. "Oh dear. I wish it were that easy," she said.

Now, I saw Wanda's family watching me, their eyes beginning to grow doubtful, almost embarrassed, as if I had said something kind of dirty. I rushed on. "Some people have to hide themselves from view, and they call it `being in the underground.'" I said it wasn't only criminals either but good people as well, just normal, everyday people, people I knew. Then I stopped because the adults had taken to looking at each other, rolling their eyes.

Then Mr. Thomas squinted at me and asked, "Just who are these here people you *know,* little missy?"

But already I knew I had gone too far. I had almost said stuff I knew should stay inside the family. My mother lowered her voice even inside our own house when she talked about their friends who were living "underground."

"I don't know," I mumbled.

Her father smirked. "Don't be such a smarty pants then. Now y'all run along and leave the grown-ups some peace."

I realized too late that they didn't want to be corrected by a child. And although I knew secrets they would never know, it didn't make me feel like a smarty-pants; it made me sad. For a moment, I had felt so comfortable with them that I had spoken freely, without thinking, without screening my thoughts first. I had stepped out of my ten year old self and entered into a conversation like I did at home, and I felt that I had come close to betraying family secrets. I wondered what they would do if they knew about the California phone calls. Would they want to shoot at us like we did the imaginary North Koreans in our vacant lot each evening? I put down my paper dolls and told Wanda it was time for me to go home.

I found my mother in the kitchen wrestling with the ancient washer that leaked water all over the floor every time she did the laundry. She had a mop in one hand and was trying to get the thing to stop jumping around the kitchen. Her hair hung in damp tendrils down her neck, and her cheeks had turned pink, making her seem somehow younger. It reminded me of the way she looked when she danced around the living room in Chicago, her head back, her hair swinging wildly. Today, she had on one of Walter's old tee shirts, her usual housework clothing. I never really understood why she couldn't wear normal dresses when she did housework, like my friend's mothers did. Why couldn't she wear high heels sometimes when she dusted or vacuumed, instead of old raggedy bedroom slippers?

I walked up to stand beside her and began playing absently with the soapsuds bubbling up from the machine. "Don't lean on the machine," she said, her eyes cross.

"How long are we going to live like this?" I asked her.

She stopped dead still, bent over the machine like the question had caught her in the stomach. "God, I don't know," she said. She looked like she might cry, so I wandered back outside.

We all went around that winter with runny noses. Aunt Marjorie said our blood had thinned living in California. But my mother said it was because we were living on cement over bare ground. The tar papered house rocked in the wind, and the cold became a constant enemy seeping in through the drafty windows, pushing up through the ground. Even our Korea games ended earlier.

One night, Walter came in the door smiling. That was odd because we didn't smile much anymore. He cleaned his shoes off by the back door and then brought a glass over and set it on the kitchen table. He nodded to me where I stood next to my mother at the kitchen stove. I often stood there while she cooked, as if my very presence could hurry the arrival of food. I went to the table and looked into the bowl. There on a tiny fake lily pad sat an even tinier turtle. "Maybe you can start having turtle races again," he said.

Turning her head, my mother frowned and curled her lip at him. "He smells bad," she said.

He did smell, but he brought a kind of comfort with him. He smelled earthy, like breathing California. I named him Churchy La Femme after the turtle in Pogo, our favorite comic strip. Under his hard shell, he had a soft pretty place, speckled with yellow and nice to stroke, cool like a pale green leaf.

One particularly cold night late in November, I brought him out to watch us play Korea, and when I went into bed, I forgot to bring him in. The next morning, I had just gone into the kitchen to stand in front of the oven like I usually did when Walter came in the back door from his shift carrying the turtle bowl. "You left Churchy out all night," his tone accused me.

Suddenly, I was afraid to move any closer. "Is he ok," I asked.

Walter dropped the bowl onto the kitchen table. "What do you think?" he said, his voice cold with disgust and he left the room.

I could just see the turtle from where I still stood by the stove. He looked all right, the same light green color. I went closer. Churchy looked exactly the same except that he hadn't moved I picked up a kitchen spoon. Somehow, I was afraid to touch him with my fingers like I had been doing for weeks, taking him out of his bowl and putting him around the house to delight Burr or horrify my mother. But now, when I prodded him gently with the tip of the spoon, nothing happened. My mother had come into the kitchen, and she looked down into the bowl too. "Frozen," she said. "He froze to death."

Just like the Little Match Girl, I thought, in a story we had read back in Chicago about a little beggar girl who's forced to sleep outside and freezes in the cold, cold winter night. Then I remembered the greasy boy in California and the grand turtle race. I felt tears start to form, but I blinked them back. "Just a dumb ol' turtle," I told her.

"I'm surprised at you," she said. "I thought you would have taken better care of your little friend."

I picked up Churchy's bowl and took him into my room. I might have cried freely in front of them back in Chicago, or even in California, but now, something seemed to be clogging my throat, and I didn't feel the same about crying in front of my parents any more. There didn't seem to be any room available for grief.

Instead, I spent all morning shut up in my room with some books, thinking of Grandma's dead baby boys turned into angels, and writing out Churchy's funeral. When I finally got dressed and went outside, some kids were already out in the field playing Korea, so I went and got Wanda. We made a pulpit out of orange crates. For once, my mother didn't give a lecture on the futility of religion. Instead, she let me bring our wooden kitchen chairs out to the mud yard. Even though it was cold, and we could see our breath in the air, some of the other kids drifted over to the funeral site, and by the time we had the turtle laid out in his cigar box draped with a piece of an old dusting rag contributed by Mary Louise, a lot of the neighborhood was out in the lot waiting for the funeral.

I pulled out my notebook, and everyone quieted down. I looked out over my audience, seeing them expectant like something important might be going happen. My heart started pounding, and my mouth felt like it had sand stuck inside. But when I began to read, I felt them grow still, felt them listening. I paused and looked up toward our house to see if my mother had come out. I had borrowed a lot of words directly from *The Grapes of Wrath*, and mixed them with my own. I thought probably they'd recognize them and be proud of me for using one of their favorite authors. My mother and Walter had both come out, and they stood together on the stoop, my mother holding Burr, who still managed to wave his fist at me, despite being bundled in blankets. But if they recognized their hero's words, they didn't let on.

When I finished, I looked up. My friends sat very quietly. I saw Mary Louise, sitting in the front row next to Wanda, reach up and wipe her eyes. Wanda, fidgeting in her seat, watched her, looking worried. But I was ecstatic. My words, I thought, had made her cry! And even my parents, standing there in the chilly late afternoon sun, looked, I thought, properly sad.

One night after Walter left for work, Burr woke me crying out like he often did in the night. Most of the time, he went back to sleep in a minute or two. Lately, he had been fretful with a cold. When he kept on fussing, making a strange croaking sound, I got up and went into the living room. He looked pitiful lying there, his blankets all twisted around him, his face red. I lifted him out of bed and sat down with him in the rocking chair. This usually soothed him, and my mother spent a lot of time rocking and singing lullabies or just staring off into space. So I rocked him like Aunt Marjorie had rocked me that first night in Denver. But he wouldn't stop crying no matter what I did. I jiggled him on my shoulder like I'd seen my mother do when he had a stomachache. Then I laid him across my lap, and his body burned into my legs through the blankets. Not knowing what else to do, I kept rocking and singing my mother's lullabies, and after awhile, his cries became more like whimpers. After awhile, I began to cry with him, thinking about the baby uncles, flying up to heaven with their tiny wings. We must have cried ourselves to sleep.

When I woke up the next day, I was in my own bed. They told me Burr had gone to the hospital with pneumonia; they told me they had to pry him out of my arms that I wouldn't let go as if I had been afraid we might never get him back. And we almost didn't.

He spent the next weeks in isolation. We bought an old car to get back and forth to the hospital, and then stood helplessly outside the window, watching him lying in his oxygen tent. He could see us through the glass and cried for us, but they wouldn't let us near him. Back at home, it seemed strangely quiet without him, the empty rocking chair in the corner a constant reminder.

They brought him home on a dismal day that turned our mud yard into icy ruts. I rushed to the door when I heard the old car they had bought in order to get back and forth to the hospital. My mother came in carrying Burr in her arms. They were both crying, but in my excitement at seeing him, I barely noticed their tears, and I reached out my arms expecting him to laugh and throw himself on me like usual. But his little face was pinched and white, and he just stared at me. Something sad and empty about his eyes reminded me of the pictures we had seen of European war orphans. I touched him gently on the arm, and he pulled himself back from my touch, turning his head away, his face turned toward my mother, staring at her, searching her face, his eyes bewildered.

"Mama," I whispered, "he's forgotten who we are."

I came home from school to find my mother waving the mop while the washing machine cheerfully bubbled over onto the floor. "Guess what?" she asked the second I came through the door, her eyes dancing. I couldn't imagine what could have caused this sudden mood swing. "Paul Robeson's coming!"

"Here?" Incredulous, I looked around our living room, still empty except for Burr's crib and toys lying everywhere like cuddly land mines.

"No, Silly. Here in Denver. Just imagine! We'll be able to hear *our* music for a change."

It struck me...our music. I thought about how she always sang along with him with tears in her eyes when Paul Robeson sang, "We must keep fightin' until we're dyin'...." on our record player back in Chicago.

"It's unbelievable," my mother shook her head, her eyes serious again, "a man with a voice that inspired Jerome Kern to write "Old Man River," can't even sell records in his own country, but has to go to Europe to make a living!"

"Are we going?" I asked. We never went anywhere.

"You bet we are," she said. "They say this may be his last concert ever in the United States. Looks like his criticism of the scoundrels in Washington and their dirty cold war policies has cost him his living."

But I was lost in my own memories, being sung to sleep with "My Curly Headed Baby" coming softly through the slice of dark that separated my Chicago bedroom from the grown up world just beyond the open sliding door.

Not since Chicago had we sat with such a crowd of people, waving and smiling at one another. Aunt Marjorie sat next to my mother, who held Burr while Walter sat on the end. "Who would have thought there were this many progressive people in Denver," my mother said.

"Most of them are in this room," said Aunt Marjorie. She looked around, recognizing and waving to some people. "If the F.B.I. wanted to clean us out, all they'd have to do is drop one little bomb right over this auditorium."

"Seems like a simpler plan than the one they've got," said my mother.

I twisted in my seat to look around the room. I saw kids, some babies, an old couple holding hands, some men in overalls like grandpa always wore, young women in kerchiefs, a bunch of teenagers giggling in one corner, and people of all shades of brown, laughing and talking among themselves. I looked, but I didn't see any men like the ones who had driven by on El Segundo Boulevard, serious men in wide brimmed hats.

Then I heard my aunt ask my mother quietly, "Are you?"

I turned toward them knowing instantly, not even sure how I knew. "You're pregnant," I said, and I heard my voice, hard and flat, accusing her.

"Yes," my mother said, frowning like she had caught my tone of voice.

I remembered her lying in her bedroom in California, hot and whiny, like a baby herself. "Oh no!"

"It was an accident," she said and tightened her mouth against me.

An *accident?* Having a baby wasn't an accident like spilling milk, like accidentally bumping something. Having a baby was serious. It meant months in bed; it meant crying and being sick all the time. While we waited for the concert, all I could think about was how hard it would be here in Denver with no grandma to bake oatmeal bread and cook potatoes and gravy? *It would all be up to me,* I thought. And I didn't see how I could do it. I felt my heart harden against them.

When at last the curtain rose, and Paul Robeson stepped out onto the stage, he took over the room. My pain quickly ebbed, becoming part of the sound. I forgot about everything but the music. His voice poured into the air, a thick, warm blanket of sound that covered me and comforted me and took me back to the big chair in our living room in Chicago. When he sang "Old Man River," I peeked at my mother and sure enough she had tears in her eyes, so I held onto her hand till the song was over. Then she leaned down and whispered our secret Chicago pledge: "If you love me and don't want to say so, squeeze my hand." I squeezed hard, my hard heart melting a little.

At the end of the program, black men and women walked out onto the stage to join Robeson singing "Freedom Train," and the audience rose to its feet and joined in. I found myself singing even though I didn't know all the words, but I didn't care. Something soothing in this crowd made it possible for the words to come out right anyway. "I'm in love again," my mother said over the music. I wasn't sure what she meant, but it sounded odd because although we talked *about* love in my family, we never said it directly. Even when Grandma used to go around saying, "I love all of my descendants," it sounded more like science than anything I could take personally. My mother used even more public expressions of love, saying things like, "I love all of mankind," or "according to Marx, `Love is the greatest thing on earth.'" But just the thought of anyone looking directly at me and saying, "I love you" made me squirm. The closest we got was squeezing hands.

People began turning around to smile at one another. Soon they started reaching across aisles and over the backs of chairs until everyone was holding hands and singing. The walls seemed to move with the sound, rising until the final burst crashed into silence. Everyone remained standing, unable to move, waiting. Then Paul Robeson stepped forward. "My friends..." he began, and the magnificent voice broke and was silent. He stood perfectly still for a moment, his head bent like he might be praying, and the silence grew around us and inside us, more powerful even than the music had been. Then he leaped from the stage and began moving among us, touching everyone as he went. Arms reached out, hands grasped, held, moved away. New hands took their place, brown and white hands, reaching, stretching, and it was all feeling and smiling and crying at the same time. It felt like it would last forever.

But it was 1952, and out in the parking lot, a man in a grey raincoat was strolling through the rows of cars and taking down the license plate numbers.

My mother was away at work about a week later, and I was trying to finish eating my chicken. When Walter cooked chicken he managed to burn it on the outside while still leaving it partially raw inside. Suddenly, as if he had just made the decision, Walter said I should finish up because we were going to visit some old friends who lived nearby. I hadn't known they had any friends here, but Walter mumbled something about how the concert made them realize how isolated we had been.

I tried to picture the place we were going. Would there be food? While I stuffed Burr into his snowsuit, I imagined it: French fried potato sticks like the ones I had stuffed myself with back in Chicago, or chocolate chip cookies like Kay's mother used to make, or maybe even tortillas like Mary Louise's mother made. I had a limited imagination for party food. Now that Walter did some of the cooking, our meals had not improved. He, too, depended on eggs or the half raw chicken legs, and filled it out with some kind of watery frozen vegetables that tasted more like vegetable-flavored Popsicles.

It was starting to snow lightly when we started out. Burr chased the flakes, and Walter and I swung him between us. I could feel the cold making my cheeks tingle. By the time we got to their house, we all felt quite jolly. But as soon as we walked in their front door, I knew it was a mistake. I could smell rejection a mile away.

A lot of people sat crowded into a small living room sipping drinks and eating nuts and candy out of little glass bowls. The house had the look of a birthday party, except that a curious tension floated in the air. Everyone stopped talking when we came in, as if we had interrupted something. Then a man rushed over and shook Walter's hand solemnly as if we were strangers being welcomed to a strange land. His wife rushed up and took our coats smiling the whole time and saying, "Well now, *this* *is* a surprise!" in the tone of voice my mother used when she reported some national crisis. While Walter, never good at small talk, smiled and shuffled his feet, I stood around hanging onto Burr, who was determined to get at the bowls of candy and wishing I were someplace else. This was just another place, I thought, to feel left out of. I don't even remember if we got any food. We didn't stay long.

Walking home that night, Walter carried the sleeping baby, and we said little to each other. Walter broke the silence once, saying quietly,

"Guess I should have warned them." *Warned them?* I thought. Like we had some horrible disease that people might need to protect themselves against. How could the three of *us* contaminate a whole roomful of people?

It had turned colder and was still snowing. We walked silently through the dark streets. I had forgotten my gloves, so I crammed my hands into my pockets and tucked my chin down inside my coat collar. The snow kept on falling, muffling our steps, the dark covering us, hiding us from the world and from each other.

Walter stood in the kitchen still wearing his jacket. His face looked caved in, like the muscles had all gone slack. My mother sat at the kitchen table, her head leaning into her hand. She sat much too still, and she stroked the hair along her forehead. She watched Walter's face like she was waiting for a sign. Alert to the sudden shift in the air, I stood by the table, feeling the atmosphere roll and change color. "I should have known that night we went visiting," Walter said, "the way even those folks acted scared and embarrassed at the same time. He's a union steward; he knew something was up."

"How could they fire you for resting for a few minutes when everyone does it?" my mother asked.

Walter shrugged. "Some of them take actual cat naps. They just roll up the rubber pallets and snooze. I can't imagine how anyone even saw me way off in that corner where they stuck me. That should have been the first warning when they took me off my regular job and got me stacking rubber off by myself." My mother had slumped further down on the chair. Walter went on almost like he was talking to himself. "Or when Jose stopped being friendly. That was a sign that something was up." Jose, Mary Louise's father, had shared rides with Walter. They had been friends ever since Walter, acting as shop steward, had helped him settle a grievance. Walter told us how some of the guys went around saying "they didn't want to work next to no damn Mexicans." As shop steward, Walter had treated them all the same.

All I knew was when I played at Mary Louise's house, I left stuffed with wonderfully spicy food. Even now my stomach growled just thinking about the home-made tortillas that sat on their kitchen counter in a bowl covered by a white dish towel. We kids just ran in from outside whenever we felt hungry and there they'd be like magic, hot and doughy and warm in the stomach like a sunny day.

"I should have known," he went on, "because Jose barely talks to me these days, like I meant trouble for him, might even cause him to lose his new job." He didn't say this bitterly, like he blamed Jose, just as a matter of fact, like it couldn't be helped, like it was sure as rain.

"You can appeal to the union," said my mother.

"I'll appeal, but it won't do any good. The union's too chicken these days to back me up. The other union steward, the one we all thought was bucking for foreman, has been turning his head away when he sees me coming. He knew the ax was going to fall."

My mother pushed herself out of her chair. "Oh, I can't stand it. We used to be union organizers, and now we can't get the union to do for us what we've done for others. It's more than I can stand, more than anyone should have to bear." Her voice had risen at the end. And as if her rising anger had given her sustenance, I saw her back stiffen and come away from the back of the chair. Walter turned his head and watched her, but he didn't say anything. Their fear floated right on past me. I felt a curious surge of nervous energy. I was beginning to understand that while crying didn't help much, anger could get things going.

When the letter came a few weeks later, I was ready. My grandmother wrote to tell us they were looking for a principal of the grade school in a town near their ranch in the Ozarks. She wrote: "You can stay on our ranch while you get settled. There's a vegetable garden and healthy cows, Nellie, Bessie and Molly, and you'll all love these fine southern people. Love, Mocky. P.S. Tell Christine we have a horse, too."

"Let's go," I said, not even caring where the Ozarks were, just hoping they were some place away from heartbreak.

"Maybe it's the chance we need," said my mother. She was looking out of the window at the spring thaw. Something strange had happened to the mud lot where we had held our war games. At first we had noticed only tiny green shoots, and then one day my mother had looked out of the window in the middle of our oatmeal and burst out laughing. "My God," she said, "take a look. We've been living in a cabbage patch." When I got up and went over to the window, my eyes followed her finger pointing out where row after row of tiny leaves curled around each other, like embryo cabbages. Just then the landlord come out of his back door, and strode across his field carrying his hoe like a sword.

As we were leaving Denver, Mamie and Dwight Eisenhower were arriving to visit her parents at their Denver home. "Maybe we should drop in and say goodbye," said my mother over the top of the newspaper with a flash of her old humor. The night before we left, we heard Joe McCarthy on the radio saying that General MacArthur was the greatest American ever born and then went on to talk about the number of square miles the "commie-loving Democrats" had turned over to the Kremlin."

When I asked my mother what it meant, she shushed me, and then we heard McCarthy say something about the "slimy traitors who had slithered into the Red-Dean's State Department." He said he would be presenting the American people with charts and graphs to prove his allegations soon. My mother looked grim. "He could be pulling out his laundry list for all we know," she said. "No one has the guts to check anything that maniac says when he points his diabolical finger at someone...at everyone."

The day we left, the sun shone bright and hot. As we stuffed the last of our raggedy belongings into my uncle's car, the landlord come out into the middle of his patch. He spent most of his time these days digging around the neat rows of baby cabbages, and whenever we left the house, he'd be out there, leaning on his hoe, his eyes narrowed, watching us like he knew something about us, like he knew we might be dangerous. I could feel my insides kind of clench under the force of his eyes, but my mother would toss her head and smile daggers, her eyes full of blood. "He doesn't like anyone," she said. "especially Mexicans *and* Communists."

Today, he was leaning on his hoe, watching. My mother waved gaily, but he didn't respond. "Too bad we're leaving just as its getting pretty," she said, sweeping her arm across the entire field. But I knew she didn't mean it. We were all glad to be leaving this cold, mean place. It had been the hardest place to live and the easiest to leave. But if I had known then what was still ahead, I might have dragged my feet a bit more, might have been less anxious to fly off into the unknown.

Then someone called out, "Wait," and we all turned to see Mary Louise and her mother hurrying along the street toward us. Mrs. Juarez held something clutched to her chest. Mary Louise ran right up to me, and we hugged each other. Mrs. Juarez held out a bowl covered with a white dishtowel toward my mother. She was smiling softly, like she felt shy about her gift. My mother took the bowl. Walter had come over to stand next to her, and I saw his eyes roam the street down to their house where Jose stood on their porch. He waved, and Jose waved back. "Oh, I couldn't take your bowl," my mother said, holding the bowl gingerly like it might explode.

"It's ok," said Mrs. Juarez. "I have lots more of them." She looked down at me, still smiling. "I know how Christine loves tortillas." My mother pulled the bowl in closer. "Well, if you're sure."

"Yes, yes. To keep you warm." Her eyes smiled at us. Even my mother got it then, standing there in the late spring heat, 90' degrees in the shade; just what we needed, tortillas in a blue bowl under a cool white cloth to keep us warm.

As we drove away all of us waving madly, Mary Louise and I blowing kisses and Mrs. Juarez smiling, I looked out toward the cabbages for the last time. They sat quietly, even bravely in their neat rows, their green leaves curling up to the sun.

In 1953 the Firestone Tire and rubber Company discharged a worker for making provocative statements about the relative merits of the United States and the Soviet Union...
    -David Caute, *The Great Fear*

An extensive survey conducted under the direction of Professor Samuel A, Stouffer, of Harvard, and published in 1954 showed 52% of a national cross section in favor of imprisoning all Communists (other polls yielded an even higher percentage)...

But this massive intolerance was not focused on Communists alone: 45% would not allow Socialists to publish their own newspapers, and 42% wanted to deny the press the right to criticize the "American form of government."

Yet only 3% of Souffer's national cross section claimed ever to have met an avowed Communist...

He was always talking about world peace.
(Housewife in Oregon.)
I saw a map of Russia on a wall in his home.
(Locomotive Engineer, Michigan)
Just his slant on community life and church work.
He brought a lot of foreign looking people into his house. (Housewife, Kansas.)
    -David Caute, *The Great Fear*

Julius and Ethel Rosenberg were executed on June 19, 1953

ARKANSAS, 1953

Just east of the Oklahoma border, we reached Huntington, Arkansas. I pressed my face to the car window as we drove past the movie theater, the dry goods store, post office and drug store, then on down the street where the bank and the grain mill marked the edge of town. There the gravel road left the town and zigzagged back through the pine covered hills where the temperature hovered at 105', baking the earth into clay bricks, and blowing the red earth hot and dry across the road. It covered our car in a fine red dust.

About 5 miles outside of town, the car sputtered to a stop. "Oh no," my mother said from the back seat, her voice a paler thinner voice. Walter got out and opened up the hood, and then because the heat was killing us, we all spilled out and stood in the gravel by the side of the road. We took a breath of hot air and got our bearings. Tall pines towered dense and dark on either side of the road that stretched out in both directions, deserted and silent, as if even sound itself had been muffled by the shimmering heat. My mother kind of shivered and wrapped her arms around herself. Her dress was dark with sweat where Burr had leaned against her. "Where's everyone?" I asked. It didn't seem possible a road could be so empty.

"I expect a vigilante group will ride up any minute and carry us off," she said.

Walter, seemingly unruffled by the silent heat, said, "We need to phone for help."

"A phone? Out here in the sticks?" She looked around incredulously. "Fat chance." Just then there were car sounds in the distance. "Here comes the posse," she said.

I expected cowboy hats, men on horseback-certainly not the old car coming ever so slowly toward us. We must have been a strange sight standing alongside the road, all wrinkled and sweaty looking, like we just dropped out of the sky. Burr who had been playing in the gravel was already covered in a fine coat of the strange red dust. My mother picked him up and ran a finger along one of Burr's little arms. "This dirt," she said, "isn't even the proper dirt color."

The car slowed to a stop, and a little wizened man in a white shirt and a grey fedora stuck his head out of the window. "Y'all got car trouble?" he asked.

Walter came around our car, smiling in a friendly way. "We've just driven in from Denver," he said, "and we're looking for my father-in-law Clare Christie's ranch."

The man looked momentarily startled, then he motioned with his head. "Y'all best git in, and I'll just carry y'all over there."

We got in. The hot car felt almost cool after the road. Walter introduced us and for a change, he did all the talking. My mother sat silently next to me in the back seat, a damp, faded version of herself. The car jolted forward, and then crawled down the road. I had never imagined a car could go that slow.

"Y'all new to these parts," the man said, a statement not a question.

"Do you know my father-in-law, Clare Christie?" Walter asked.

The man took his eyes off the road a moment to look at Walter; then he smiled. "I know Mr. Christie's more ambitious than most. Why, I hear tell he has melon planted this year." He nodded to Walter, as if waiting for him to acknowledge this amazing feat. But no one knew how to respond. I was fascinated by the soft sound his words made. Compared with him, Walter's voice suddenly sounded hard.

It felt like hours, sitting crammed in the hot back seat, but finally, we came around a bend in the road and the man slowed even more and pointed. I could just make out Grandma standing on the edge of the road, her hands over her eyes, peering down the road at our car coming toward her. I barely noticed that she stood in front of a grey shingled lean-to. But my mother leaned forward on the seat and took it all in. She saw the tiny logger's cabin tilting toward the screened in porch, sitting in a sea of uncut, dry grass. I heard her indrawn breath as her eyes took in the dense scrub pine that stretched up into the red clay hills. She sagged back against the seat. "My God," she said, "so *this* is the ranch."

Then my grandmother started toward the car, smiling and holding out her arms, and I, barely waiting for the car to stop, hurled myself out the door and into them. "My darlings are here at last," said Grandma, looking so delighted to see us that for a moment I forgot we had landed on still another strange planet.

Walter and grandpa stood outside near the car instead of hurrying inside. They stood around in the long grass talking about crops and weather, while the rest of us banged in through the screen door and sort of settled ourselves.

My mother, Walter and Burr took the one tiny bedroom off the living room. It had bare wood walls and a faded linoleum floor like the rest of the house. The central room held an old couch, a rocking chair, a reading lamp next to grandma's basket of crocheting, and in the center, a wooden kitchen table surrounded by four chairs. I couldn't help wondering where we would all sit. My grandparents had already moved their bed and dresser to the makeshift back porch, and I put my few belongings under the cot made up for me at one end of the kitchen.

In that kitchen, it could have been 1900 instead of 1952. An old porcelain sink hung off the back of the kitchen with one faucet of cold running water. If we wanted hot water, it had to be heated on the big wood cook stove at the other end of the kitchen. One of grandma's endless chores was to keep a fire going most all day to boil water for washing dishes and cooking our meals. She kept a metal stoker hooked into a burner lid, so she could lift it and poke around the coals. By mid afternoon, the temperature in that kitchen hovered around 120'.

Several hours after we arrived, I had to take my first official trip to the outhouse. It sat at the far end of a dirt path, halfway out to the barn, a good distance from the back of the cabin. "Your grandfather is very particular about his outhouses," said my grandmother as if he had been doing nothing all these years but designing outhouses. "He builds them a good ways from the well and keeps them sterile with lots of lime, so you skedaddle right on out there and do your business."

At first, it seemed like an adventure to meander down the grassy path towards a tiny wooden house. When I opened the door of the rough wooden shed, the smell assaulted me. I covered my nose and went slowly in, keeping the door open as long as I could. But then the door banged behind me, and it was dark inside except for the slivers of light coming in through the hole in the door and the cracks along the wooden sides. The floor felt gritty under my feet. I stood still, trying not to breathe, while my eyes adjusted to the dark. I could make out cobwebs hanging in the corners along the rough planks. Then I forced myself to look down one of the holes. To my horror, I saw a huge pile of turds of varying shades of brown, some dry and covered with lime like pale frosting. One neat mound looked damply fresh like it might have been put there only minutes ago. I held my hand over my mouth and nose and stared down into the hole in stunned fascination.

Suddenly, the turds moved and a turtle stuck up its huge head above the muck. I plunged out of the door and went screaming back up the path. "Here, here," said Grandpa, as I came past the pump house, "what's all this noise about?" He was standing outside the back door with his old grey hat pushed back on his head, as if to see me better.

"Grandpa, there's a real turtle in there," I screeched," He'll die in all that poop. We've got to get him out."

Grandpa flinched as my voice rose louder and shriller at the end. "He lives there," he said quietly.

"Lives there?" I stopped, aghast. "How could he?"

Grandpa leaned down and spit a long, brown stream of tobacco juice. "Just does. We live in here," he gestured up toward the house, "and he lives in there. Guess he likes shit."

That first night as I lay on my cot in the kitchen, the dark came alive with wings. Pale green wings beat at the screens, wings as fine as gossamer fluttered above my head. The air sang. Colonies of long brown creatures with legs like bent sticks covered the light in the ceiling, casting tiny shadows on the walls, making the walls move. "Turn off the light, little darling," called grandma from the back porch. "Don't you see they're attracted to the light."

But I couldn't move. Seeing them was better than hearing them and wondering where they might land. Most of them seemed happy to flutter along the walls and the ceiling, but occasionally, one landed on the bed with a gentle plopping sound, and I yelped and jumped and flung out my arms to push it away. Every now and then grandma called in, her voice heavier and heavier with sleep, "Go to sleep. Nothing's going to hurt you." Finally, I pulled the sheet up over my mouth, covering everything except my eyes. I lay in a pool of light, sweating and praying for morning while the night hummed gently around me, and grandpa and grandma snored in unison from the back porch.

My mother couldn't wait to get out of the cabin. As soon as she and Walter and grandpa finished first shift at the breakfast table, they went off to find us a place to live in the nearby town where Walter had been hired to be principal of the grade school. I was left to follow my grandparents around. After a while, I got tired of watching my grandmother washing the dishes in the porcelain dishpan or making bread like she had done back in Chicago, although here the task seemed endless, coupled with stoking the fire, feeding the cats, and starting the meat for dinner. I could wander outside and read on the porch where the temperature went from 120' to a cooler 100'.

Every day about noon, grandpa came in for dinner, the biggest meal of the day. Usually my grandmother cooked some kind of meat, mostly hamburger or chicken, made potatoes, either boiled or mashed and several of the vegetables growing outside in their garden. Then the cabin became unbearable in the heat from the wood cook stove, and grandpa lay on the couch with a wet rag over his head. About 1:00 p.m. he sat up, pulled his pant leg up and began rubbing his left leg, which was nearly black from the knee to the ankle. "Aches like the toothache," he'd say. After a few minutes, he'd heave himself off the couch, put on his hat with the sweat stain around the brim, and go back out to the barn to swat flies off the horse for awhile.

They called the big brown workhorse Jackson after the town in Michigan where Grandpa said he went to "raise Hell" when he was a boy. Hearing my grandfather say those words gave me a thrill. While my mother and grandmother dwelt in the land of fairy tales, making their make-believe world as common place as table salt, my grandfather could make the ordinary lives of men exotic and exciting. I imagined him as a young man riding bareback on a horse like Jackson, riding through town whooping and hollering like I'd heard my great grandfather had done. Aunt Marjorie told my mother it was a disgrace how her grandfather got so drunk they had to bring him home lying across the back of his horse. But I expected Grandpa had been cut from tougher cloth. He always said about his father-in-law, "That little banty Irishman never got the goods on me." In my eyes, Jackson, the horse, took on the sheen of my grandfather's manhood.

Grandpa said he didn't much care about Jackson one way or the other. But my mother said that was nonsense. "Why would you stand there swatting flies off something you didn't like?"

First thing, Grandpa taught me how to slide myself up on Jackson's back. We walked around the field next to the barn, Grandpa leading him by the harness and surveyed our five acre kingdom. On the other side of the road, I could see the cows grazing peacefully on an acre of cleared pasture surrounded by seventy-five acres of dense timber. I hardly ever ventured over where the tall pines stood, dark and forbidding against the cloudless sky. They seemed to come from a fairy tale, so thick and dark that a kid could get lost and never come back. And I didn't quite trust the cows either, even though Grandma had named one Molly in honor of the lost leper doll. Cows had sad eyes, I thought. I preferred the other side where Grandpa raised his vegetables, where Jackson lived in a big, ramshackle barn.

But my horse rides always ended before I was ready to let go when Grandpa said, "Jackson's not a toy. He works hard and deserves some peace and quiet. If you want to help, swat some flies." I'd swat for about five minutes, while Jackson stood patiently, his broad back shiny with sweat. Then, bored and hot, I'd go back up the path to hang out with the big yellow cats by the pump house.

On Sundays, the whole house smelled of talcum powder. Grandma put on a nylon dress, her pearls and a pair of squat heeled pumps. Then she'd color her cheeks bright pink, take a large puff and blot on powder, starting with her face, moving down to her neck and arms, while the white powder drifted along the dresser, falling until it covered the floor in a fine, white dust. Finally, she came out of the bedroom and asked, "Who's seen my black pocketbook?" After someone found the pocketbook behind a pillow on the sofa or up on top of the refrigerator, she stuffed a clean hanky and her compact inside, took a last look at herself in the old mirror and sailed out the door, her eyes rounder and brighter. Then she settled herself in the old Plymouth where Grandpa sat waiting at the wheel wearing his good grey hat and a clean shirt. She laughed and chattered like a girl going to a party, while Grandpa sat quietly resigned to his fate. He complained, "When Mocky goes anywhere, she talks to every single human being she sees, and inside of five minutes, she tells them her whole damn history." The only places I ever saw her go were shopping and church on Sunday.

One Saturday, we all slouched out to the screened porch right after breakfast while the early morning dip in temperature made the heat almost bearable. Grandma sat in her rocker fanning herself with an old *Reader's Digest*, and my mother sat across from her trying to dress Burr who wiggled to get free.

Grandma said, "Let her come to church if she wants to. If Walter is going to be principal of a school down here, he needs to put on a good face." I had asked her earlier if I could come along. Anything had to be a relief from broiling hot boredom.

My mother frowned. "Doesn't mean we should have to become hypocrites."

"O fiddle, faddle." Grandma said, "a little church never hurt anyone." She turned her face up to catch the breeze from her magazine.

"If I can stand it," said Grandpa, "anyone can."

"I expect we'll all have to learn to sing religious hymns," said Walter coming out with his coffee, giving my mother a wicked grin, then winking at me, as if to include me because it seemed usually once they got started arguing, they forgot all about me. I held onto one of Burr's arms, while my mother pulled an undershirt over his head.

"It's going to be beastly hot today. Too hot for clothes," said my grandmother.

"Don't worry about it!" snapped my mother. "You want him to get bit to death?"

"Fiddlesticks!" said grandma again, her face red now.

"Do they sing in church?" I asked, remembering when I had tried to sing with the others in school in Denver, but I didn't know the songs the other kids took for granted, so I kept making mistakes, feeling worse and worse until I had stopped singing and mouthed the words instead.

"Hold him still," said my mother. Burr had his eye on Grandpa's tobacco juice can. My mother made a gesture of distaste with her mouth. "Who knows what they sing? This church stuff makes me wonder what we're doing here."

"Trying to stay alive," said my grandfather. "This might be your one and only job offer."

"I can't understand why *you* go, dad. You don't believe any of that hogwash."

"I go so Mocky can get the gab out of her system, and so I can have some peace at home." He spit into his can and Burr lunged for it, but I grabbed him in time.

"They sing about love," said my grandmother.

"Oh. *Love.*" My mother spit it out like a bad word. "Their idea of love isn't very useful for working people who are poor as church mice."

In the end, she decided I could go. "Don't let them brainwash you," she called through the screened door as we got in the car.

"I won't," I promised.

When Grandma and I settled into the front seat, it felt like she and I were going off on an adventure together, maybe running away from home. She leaned down and kissed the top of my curls. "My little sweetheart," she murmured.

At first, I kind of liked church. I didn't even mind sitting still for an hour in the hot pew while the minister got more and more worked up about sin, a word we seldom used. I had heard my mother say, "Sin is anything the working class does to have some fun. But when the rich do the same thing, they look the other way."

At the end of the sermon, they passed around a tray of grape juice in tiny paper cups. I smiled at the man holding the tray covered with a white cloth like Mrs. Juarez's tortillas. I drank mine with relish and politely asked if I could have another. The man holding the tray started, looking shocked like I had said a bad word, and Grandma leaned down and whispered, "Shh. I'll tell you later."

On the way home, Grandma explained how the juice and cracker wasn't meant as refreshment, but rather, symbolized the blood and body of Jesus Christ. I remembered Jesus from our talks in Chicago, but I still couldn't understand why they'd want to eat someone they seemed to love so much. "Because they're foolish," said Grandpa and spit out the window.

Grandma looked at me, her eyes tender and said, "Remember Jesus loved the little children." It was the same thing they had said earlier that morning in Sunday school where I had made my next mistake.

They sat the kids at a long table and gave us little sheep and shepherds to cut out of squares of felt. Then we stuck the felt pieces around on a big board while the teacher told us the story about how Jesus got born. I loved the felt figures, and I had enjoyed the story until I tried to place the baby Jesus riding on one of the little sheep, and a kid told the teacher who had looked at me over her glasses and frowned. I knew I had done something wrong, so I laid him back down in the rough straw. I felt the familiar sting of being new, of having to go around guessing about things everyone else seemed to know already.

The best part of the summer was learning to pee outside and meeting Brenda Owens. I loved walking out in the yard any time of day or night and just squatting down. I knew I was supposed to use the outhouse, except maybe late at night when everyone went out doors, but I hated the smell, and it didn't seem to matter out here in the middle of nowhere if you peed inside or out, just as long as you didn't do it too close to the well.

I was outside in the tall grass near the barn one day when I heard the loud rattle in the distance that meant a car was on its way. My grandmother came outside for every car, or waved out the window saying something like, "There goes the Jones. Wonder why they're going to town this time of day?" Cars came by so seldom that they became a kind of event for us all. Now, an old pickup truck came around the bend in the road, rattling and rusty and full of kids. The truck veered suddenly off the road and came to a stop on our front grass. As I came across the yard, Grandma already outside, waved her apron and called out to them, her face crinkled into laugh lines, her eyes welcoming company.

A tall gaunt man sat in the cab with a freckle faced woman holding a baby. Hanging over the sides, a passel of kids stared at me, eyes alive with curiosity. The woman waved to my grandmother who called out delightedly, "Why Pebble Owens!"

The man climbed out of the truck and the woman followed, shifting a baby up with one hand. "Hot enough for you?" asked the man.

"It's beastly," said Grandma.

"Well now," said the man. He seemed at a loss for more words. He stood there stopped over shifting something in his mouth, not actually looking at anyone.

"And this sweet thing is my granddaughter, Christine." She put an arm around me. "Christine, our neighbors, Pebble and Jeff Owens, and their lovely family." She motioned to the back of the truck, laughing. I could see she was happy to see them.

"Please to meet you," said Pebble. Her husband nodded. He seemed to be gazing out toward my grandfather's crops.

"Clare's out there planting more melon," said Grandma, and then as if he heard us, my grandfather raised an arm. He was holding a melon, big as a basketball.

Jeff Owens grinned and shook his head in rueful admiration.

"I declare," said Pebble, "Mr. Christie is somethin' else."

"You're a marvel yourself, Pebble Owens, and don't you forget it," my Grandmother said, and Pebble blushed. I knew Grandma admired Pebble. I had heard her tell my mother, "Pebble has all those kids and no money, and she keeps them clean as a whistle." Clean was still my grandmother's barometer of success.

My mother had looked puzzled as if she didn't understand my grandmother's feelings for Pebble Owens. But I was beginning to get it. I could see the admiration in the shy way Pebble looked at my grandmother and how Jeff Owens, pushed back his hat and grinned out toward my grandfather, who was leaning on his hoe in the glaring sun.

"Come on in and sit," said my grandmother turning toward the porch. The kids hadn't moved from the truck. It looked like they had forgotten all about them when Pebble turned, smiled at me and said. "Brenda Owens git on out of that truck and introduce yourself." A girl about my age with long brown bangs swung herself gracefully out of the truck bed to stand there in the brilliant sun facing me, her freckles alive, almost dancing on her face. She looked shy and excited at the same time, like meeting me was something she'd been waiting for, the real event of her summer. Later, I would remember that first day, how everything suddenly settled because right from the start, Brenda steadied me. I saw myself grow smarter, prettier mirrored in the wide blue eyes of Brenda Owens. "Hey," said Brenda "Y'all want to go pick some peanuts?"

Just before school started, we settled into the second nicest house in Mansfield, Arkansas. The superintendent, a dark, little man with a hump on his back, had the nicest house, a tall brick house just over a street or two. The day we moved in Walter told my mother it was the superintendent who had gone to bat for him. "I could tell he was impressed by my teaching recommendations from Southern Cal. The only thing was he wondered whether a man with my credentials would be happy in a small town like this."

"I don't doubt he wondered. *I* wonder if we can stand this place, and *I know* we don't have much choice."

"Let's try to stay optimistic," Walter said.

I didn't share my mother's doubts, not when I saw a real gas stove in the kitchen and hot and cold running water again. "Hmm." my mother said looking around the kitchen at the pale pink and blue wallpaper with disdain, "A pastel paradise. I'll have to see what I can do to liven this house up."

But I adored the little, white frame house, our first real house since the early California days. It had a front porch and wallpaper in every room. Its only flaw was that it didn't have a real bathroom. The man next door wouldn't let them run pipes through his land, so I had to be content with the little wooden house in a corner of the yard, papered in the same pretty pattern as the living room, and except for the familiar smell, I could almost forget it was an outhouse.

I took the bedroom with walls covered in pink flowers because it looked out onto the big yard. My new bed looked small and naked all by itself, and I pushed it over to the window, so I could pretend I was sleeping under the pine tree outside. I couldn't wait to bring Brenda here. At her house, they were almost as crowded as we had been in my grandparent's cabin. But because they had so little furniture, they had more room for kids. She and Rhonda slept together in an old bed, and baby Caroline slept on a cot on the other end of the room. J.D., the only boy in the family, had the only other bedroom all to himself. I didn't think that was fair and told her so. She just shrugged and said she'd be lonely without her sisters anyway. I day dreamed sleepovers and how Brenda's eyes would light up when she saw the wallpaper and my new bedspread. I studied the pink flowered walls, making the room seem cooler, and I saw its glory through Brenda's eyes.

But soon, I nearly forgot all about Brenda Owens and became the Class Queen. I stood in the cafeteria line behind Johnnie Lee Cross waiting for dessert, and I forgot all about those scrawny chickens I had eaten at the Owens' table. I was developing a passion for southern food, more intense than my tortilla eating days in Denver. I hadn't realized how starved I was for the taste and texture of real food. I discovered cobbler and chicken, biscuits drowning in hot gravy and more kinds of peas and beans than I had known existed on earth.

When Johnnie Cross told Mrs. Jones she made the best cobbler in Arkansas, all she said to him was, "G'wan, git Johnnie Lee Cross. Y'all don't need to think you can come around and butter me up." Maybe it was because he had known them all his life, and I was more like company, or maybe it was because my father was the principal, but they piled my bowl with sweet cherries and buttery biscuit dough right up to and overflowing the brim, while I smiled my sweet smile, my butter-wouldn't-melt-in-my-mouth smile. I learned to love the bland, salty cornbread they liked, using it to wipe up my plate, and I learned to eat my eggs fried crisp in pork fat with baking powder biscuits. My mother said, "They put a pound of butter on anything they eat. It's enough to gag a person." But all that butter slid easily down my throat. At home during scrambled egg or dried out chicken suppers, I dreamed of black eyed peas swimming in pork fat.

For the first time in my life, I felt I had real power outside the family. It showed in my walk, the way I could saunter around the playground, the way I could charge through my days. I wrote a serial about a girl detective, and it got mimeographed and passed out to the class every morning. I directed the school play, picking the kids for parts by committee as my mother suggested and practicing after school. In the winter, Walter started a girl's basketball team. I joined and amazed my family by getting up early to practice free throws. I even had a paper romance, a boyfriend with red hair who wrote me love notes, and passed them secretly through the classroom while I sat enthralled by his mystery, his freckled face, his pressed blue jeans.

At lunch, we'd all sneak over to the little restaurant where the high school kids ate and listen to "How Much is That Doggy in the Window?" and for fifteen cents we could buy a hamburger with lettuce and tomato and then eat it outside among the dogwood, sitting with friends in the grass and laughing at the boys' jokes. And if I was real lucky, one of the football players would smile at me. Then we'd saunter back across the playground, and I'd ask Walter for a nickel to spend after school, while my friends hung back shy around the principal, and I'd give him a quick hug, knowing they were watching, playing to my audience.

Then arm and arm with Martha Raye, we'd walk down Main Street on our way home in the early fall sunshine. We'd stop in the drugstore and sit at the counter, soaking up coolness, sipping cherry cokes served in ice cream glasses, kicking our feet against the tile and whispering about our "boyfriends," calling them code names. And even though I had promised myself I would never let another place capture my heart, only to watch it crack and fall apart, I was beginning to believe that this time it would last, that I could go on being the class queen and have friends and everyone would love me. My mother always said we had to change the world to make it our home, but I had decided I couldn't wait that long.

These days my mother was getting harder and harder to handle. "Maybe," I'm going to have an elephant," said my mother cheerfully to Mrs. Barns in the dry goods store one morning. "I'm certainly big enough to be carrying one."

Mrs. Barns looked away from my mother's large stomach, turned red, and changed the subject. "It sure is a pretty day," she said. They said *pretty* down here when they meant *nice*. "One day's just the like the next," my mother said. "hot and sunny." She meant boring. Then she pushed up the sleeves of her new maternity blouse, and while I smiled determinedly at everyone in the store, my mother finished her shopping with a new energy

Now that she stayed home all day like in my Perfect Mother fantasies, it should have felt more normal, but our house still seemed askew, our family tilted. For instance, she practically never wore dresses. Instead, she wore paint spattered jeans and one of Walter's old tee shirts tied around her head. Even though when she went to town she changed into her one good dress because she said, "I don't want to embarrass the Class Queen," I never quite got used to the contrast between her costumes. I worried she might forget to change someday and show up at school in an old pajama top. It kept me always just a bit on guard.

She even tried baking cookies but ended up burning them because she'd stopped to give me a lecture on The Boredom and Stupidity of Southern Life. She pulled the smoldering cookies out of the oven and viciously slammed them onto the table, angry at them for being ruined. A tiny mouse chose that moment to peek around the corner of the stove, and she shrieked, picked up the broom, and dashed toward it. The terrified mouse ran around and around the kitchen in an ever narrower circle while she chased it madly, swinging the broom down to bang the floor every couple of seconds, missing the mouse and hitting chairs and dishes. Burr had toddled to the door and began to cry. I picked him up and stood there watching her smash the kitchen, feeling a mixture of awe and disgust. Finally, just as I thought she was going to demolish the entire room, she caught it behind the stove and smashed it into the floor, giving a final cry of triumph. She paused then, breathing hard now, leaning on the broom handle. "That'll teach 'em," she said. She looked up towards us, but past us, her eyes wild, as if she saw some silent enemy lingering in the wallpaper. Then she bent down and began to gingerly nudge the mouse out onto the linoleum with the edge of the broom, while Burr turned his head away and hiccupped quietly against my neck.

If I complained, which I did more often these days, about the cluttered kitchen or Burr's toys strewn everywhere, she'd stop doing the dishes and point a yellow rubber gloved finger at me and say, "I don't know what you want. I should think it'd be enough to have me trapped at home all day, at your beck and call."

Once, I made the mistake of saying I only wanted her to try and get along.

"Get along?" she yelled. "I suppose I should learn to say 'it feels like rain' or 'sure is hot today' to someone with a name like Bessie Sue? In the first place, I do *try* to talk to these people but after weather and crops, it's all downhill. And in the second place, why for God's sake, do they have to call each other by two names?"

I winced over her use of the Lord's name in vain because down here that seemed to be one of the major sins, and secretly I'd been wishing I had two names like everyone else. I desperately wanted my new name to be Laura Sue, but I didn't have the courage to bring it up.

One day I came in from school to hear her singing from the back of the house. I knew that meant trouble, since she only sang these days when she was acting up. I put my books down on the dining room table, crowded with papers Walter hadn't finished marking. Then I went back to see what was going on. I found her in their bedroom, standing up on a wooden chair, leaning over precariously to slash fire engine red paint on the wall in front of her. She had tied her hair tied back with a dust rag, and wore one of Walter's old tee shirts covered now with splotches of deep red like dried blood. She turned to greet me. Her hair had slipped out from under the rag and stood out around her head in wisps. She looked like she might be going to lead a charge across a battlefield. Trumpets blared. "How do you like it?" she brandished the paintbrush like a lance. "It's going to be beautiful," she said, not waiting for my answer, satisfaction filling her voice. I stared at the blood red walls. She went on, "This room's big enough to take the color, and I've decided to get some sheets for the windows."

"Sheets?" I managed. "On the windows?"

"Of course. It's the latest thing in *Woman's Day*, dying sheets for curtains." She stopped and studied my face a moment. "Now, don't get that look. Try to picture the finished product."

I was trying. But I felt bewildered, like a parent faced with a recalcitrant child. All I could picture were the pale pink bedrooms with lace curtains I had seen in the Sears Roebuck catalogue, or the bedrooms of my friend's parents. Once I had been invited to Saturday lunch at my new best friend Martha Raye's house, and I had peeked into her parent's bedroom on the way into their spotless kitchen. It had been done in powder blue, blue rug, blue bedspread. They even had powder blue pillow cases. I had never seen colored pillow cases. I stood mesmerized by them, and by the lace curtain fluttering in the windows, and the palest blue lacy skirt on her mother's dust-free dressing table covered with glass bottles sparkling in the sunlight.

I just knew no one down here had ever painted a bedroom red and that the color was suspect. I remembered the newspaper headlines in California and Denver, headlines that screamed of the "Red

Menace." "It's awfully bright. Are you sure, about the sheets I mean?"

Her face fell, the light in her eyes fading. I saw her disappointment, and I felt a little stab of pity, and then anger. It didn't seem right, me playing the mean parent.

"Never mind," she said, turning back to the work at hand, leaving me to stare uneasily at the sweat stains on her tee shirt. "You'll see. Maybe I'll have an open house when it's all done and invite the Baptist Ladies in for cake and coffee. I'll serve it here in the bedroom, and I'll wear a black lace negligee and sing 'The Internationale.' That way they can take their choice: whore or Communist." She cackled up at her bloody ceiling.

I thought of Mrs. Barns in the dry goods store and the Baptist minister's wife, who dressed in lilac pinafores, and I shuddered. On my way back down the hall to the kitchen looking for something to quell my suddenly queasy stomach, I could hear the strains of an old song drifting down the hall:

"OH, there's a place in France..."

For a while after that I did try to be nicer to her. If we were eating chicken and my mother had cooked it too long, and tiny pieces of charcoal clung to the dry skin and even though I had been wishing she'd fry chicken in deep grease like Martha's mother did, when she said, "How's the chicken? Too brown?

"No, " I lied. "It's great."

In my new popularity, I could afford to be generous. I wanted to tell her I was still me and that I didn't completely believe in this southern version of myself either, even though I would have said the moon was made out of butter beans to please these people. We hadn't said the tongue-can-tell verse for a long time, and it seemed too childish now to go back to it.

The first ripple in the sea of southern sweetness came in November when our school held a mock presidential election. I didn't know what to do. In a southern town there was talk about voting for the Democrats, but my mother said Harry Truman had acted a lot like a Republican, starting "the Cold War with the Russians, and that's why they're harassing progressive people like us." She said Adlai Stevenson, the Democratic candidate, came from rich folks, and you couldn't trust him to represent ordinary people. And I didn't see how I could vote for Dwight Eisenhower, a Republican. My parents said he had been a general in the U.S. Army. Besides, we were against war because too many innocent people got killed. Like my father. But I finally resolved that if I had to vote for someone, and I didn't see how I could get away with not casting a ballot in a place where everyone knew everything, I'd have to vote for Stevenson. He seemed like a nicer man in spite of being rich.

The next morning at breakfast, I asked Walter what he was going to do. "Everyone will be watching," I reminded him.

He smiled mysteriously and said he'd think of something.

After everyone had voted, using the ballot boxes we'd made with red, white and blue crepe paper, we all filed back to our seats to wait for the votes to be counted. The classroom buzzed. Everyone acted carried as if there had been a real election, but I felt too nervous worrying about Walter's vote to join in. I had seen him briefly in the voting room, saw him fold a piece of white paper and drop it in the box before our eyes met across the room. Somehow, this seemed like some sort of test, and I couldn't imagine how it would get resolved painlessly, how Walter could participate and at the same time not betray what I knew to be his true feelings. I remembered my first election when I went out with my mother into the streets of Chicago, going door to door passing out leaflets for Henry Wallace. At home we had gone around chanting, "Two, four, six, eight, we want Wallace in '48." Now, it was 1953, and it all seemed much more complicated.

Then there was a knock on the door and a fifth grader came in carrying a sheet of paper. He handed it to Mrs. Lewis with a flourish. I held my breath while Mrs. Lewis read off the numbers. Dwight D. Eisenhower had carried our part of the Democratic South; Stevenson had trailed way behind, and Mrs. Lewis paused, her face impassive as she told us there was one vote cast for Abraham Lincoln. The kids all looked at each other, saying, "Who on earth?" But I knew who on earth, and I had to look down at my desk, so no one would see me smile.

It didn't take them very long to figure it out. A couple of days later, I heard Johnny Lee Cross ask

Billy Ray on the playground, "Who else but a Yankee would cast a vote for a nigger lover?" Only I knew it had nothing to do with being Yankees because my family did strange things no matter where we lived.

When I saw Walter on the playground at lunchtime, he winked at me. I smiled back, liking him suddenly in a new way. I felt I had been offered a kind of reprieve. We might be trying to fit in, but we hadn't, as Grandpa always said, run away with our tails between our legs.

A few weeks later, my friends and I were walking home one day, and when we got to the corner of Main Street, there she was, a black girl, maybe a little older than we were, standing on the curb with her back to us, like she might be waiting for a bus. But no buses ran in Mansfield, and I had never seen any black people around here before. It startled me, and I slowed, staring at her.

Then Sue Caroline stopped in her tracks, narrowed her pretty blue eyes and kind of flounced out her hip saying in a loud voice, "What is *she* doin' around her? Whoever does she think she is?" Her pink cheeks grew pinker as she glared at the girl's averted face. Sue Caroline sounded so mean, it made me embarrassed, but if the girl heard, she gave no sign. Her face remained still as a stone. There was not even a flicker to show she was aware of us standing there so close I could have reached out and touched her. We stood there a moment longer. Then with a shake of her blond head, Sue Caroline turned away, and we all fell in behind her. As we passed by the girl, I couldn't help noticing how straight she held her back, her shoulders pulled back ever so slightly, the tension perceptible along the delicate shoulder blades sticking out from underneath her dress. I had a sudden urge to touch her, to comfort the fear out of her straight, silent back. I had felt that fear on those smoggy mornings in California when something menacing had hovered in the air. But instead, I kept my eyes on my feet, and the soft southern breeze left a taste of dust in my mouth. We passed by, and I said nothing. But I knew I was guilty by association and by my silence.

That night at supper, my mother said, "The Class Queen is awfully quiet tonight." Usually, I went on about school, telling her every detail, but tonight I felt uneasy, as if the walk home had taken the shine off my day. Then I blurted out the incident of the black girl on the corner.

Walter put down his fork, his eyes serious. "Not too long ago," he said, "we got a shipment of new school desks, and when I wondered what to do with the old ones, one of my teachers said, 'Why don't you give them to the nigger school?' That was the first time I fully realized that all the Negro children in this county went to one school. Some of them have to travel a good distance to get there, and I also realized that their equipment is all hand-me-downs from the white schools."

"That's southern segregation for you," said my mother.

But I was still watching Walter's face. I hadn't seen that white look around his eyes since we got down here. "It bothers me," he said, "but I don't see there's anything I can do about it." For a minute no one said anything until Burr banged on the table with his spoon. Then my mother launched into one of her "I Hate Southern Life" tirades, and I tuned her out like I usually did.

But that black girl stuck in my mind like a hard, sharp stone that kept poking me. I didn't understand why I couldn't just forget about it. Why I had to keep seeing Carolyn's face, her cheeks flaming, her eyes small and mean when she looked at that black girl, just standing there on the curb paying us no mind at all. I didn't want to think about it. *I* didn't have anything to worry about. *I* wasn't black.

I just wanted to go on walking home with my friends, swinging our arms in time to the day, sauntering down the street without a care in the world. I wanted to drink cherry cokes and feel safe. I wanted to stay on the *inside* for a change.

In January, my mother went to the hospital to have the baby. I kissed her goodbye, and then, because I was leaving to go stay with Martha Raye, I went into the living room to say goodbye to the tree. Our Christmas tree still stood majestically in one corner, its branches reaching out across taking the living room. "First tree I've had from my own land since Michigan," Grandpa had said, when he dragged it into our house like a trophy. He had stuffed the huge trunk into a tree stand, anchoring the branches with rope tied to a couple of stout nails he drove into the wall behind it. Nobody could bear to throw it out.

I turned the lights on one last time. The tree sparkled all the way up to the star that touched the ceiling. Its branches seemed to gather me in. *Grandpa's tree*, I thought, *Grandpa's land*, and the thought made me feel warm, like buttei milk baking powder biscuits, like boysenberry pie.

While my mother was busy having my sister, I was living out my Perfect Family fantasies. Whatever the Raye family home might have lacked in stature, it made up for in 1950's good housekeeping. I slept with Martha in her twin bed under her pink, ruffled bedspread. In the morning, Mrs. Raye fixed us ham and biscuits and then baked chocolate chip cookies, moving cheerfully around her white kitchen wearing a gingham apron. Even the appliances wore little white cotton covers. I was in heaven. When she came in to kiss us goodnight, she gave me a sweet smile and said she hoped I didn't miss my mother "too awfully much."

"No ma'am," I told her piously, but the truth was I didn't miss her at all. I could have stayed here drowning in pink ruffles and chocolate chip cookies forever.

But on Saturday afternoon, my mother came home again, and I did too, dragging my overnight case into her bedroom, glad to see her in spite of having to leave my ideal family. She lay there in bed, her face gentler, and in the crook of her arm my new sister slept peacefully. She smiled and held out her free arm to me. "I missed you," she said.

"Me too," I lied, bending down to kiss her cheek as soft as silk. She smelled faintly medicinal with undertones of gardenia. I felt a wave of longing to have her all to myself like in our old life before babies and strange cars had changed us. As if she read my mind, the baby stirred and opened her eyes which were dark blue and still unfocused. "Brown eyes, I think," said my mother. "We named her Marjorie Edith. We wanted your grandmother's name included."

I waited for baby Marjorie to begin to cry, but instead her eyes wandered around for a moment and then came to rest on my face. She lay quietly, as if studying me. "There's your big sister," crooned my mother. Then she said with a flash of her old mischief. "Maybe we'll start calling you two Big Sister and Little Sister like your friend's family in California."

"At least she's quiet," I said, remembering how Burr had cried night and day at her age. Suddenly, I felt sorry for my sister, new to the world, still unknowing about how treacherous the world could be. "She'll find out," I said, thinking out loud.

And my mother, reading my mind like she used to, said quietly, "Yes. I suppose she'll find out soon enough."

On a chilly February day, about two weeks later Martha Raye and I were walking home from school, and just as we passed the dry goods store, I felt a shadow along the road on my right. I looked up to see a grey car slowing down as it passed us. Something about the way it seemed to slide by us made me catch my breath. As it passed, I thought I caught a glimpse of a man in a grey trench coat driving. Then it sped up and went on down the street. Martha Raye was looking at me oddly, "Why Christine, you look like you've just seen a ghost."

"Did you see that car?" I asked her,

"I didn't pay it no mind," she said, still watching my face.

I didn't say any more about it, but the rest of the way home I hoped it had been only a ghost. When I got home, still uneasy, I went looking for my mother. I found Brenda's older sister, Margie, standing in our living room, holding the baby. She smiled at me in that friendly Owens way, and my mother came in all made up and dressed in her company clothes. "Look who's come to help out with Lolly Lulu Honey," she said. She and Margie chuckled like they shared a joke together.

"Hi, Margie. Lolly who?" Even though I was glad to see Margie, I felt a little cross at my mother. I needed to talk to her about something important, and here she was all dressed up and acting jolly like she did for company.

"Margie and I have given your sister her southern name," said my mother. "We found Marjorie too dignified for someone still wetting her pants."

I heard the front door open and turned to see Walter come in. He took awhile closing the door carefully behind him. When he turned toward us, my breath caught in my throat because his face looked pale, like he might have seen a ghost. I glanced over at Margie, standing there smiling, cute as ever, then at my mother, but she was tucking in the baby's blanket and didn't seem to notice anything. "You're home early," she said. "You must have run out of papers."

I felt the air around me shift direction. Then Walter kind of shook his head and smiled at Margie. "Hello there, Margie," he said. "How's your family?"

Margie must have answered, but I didn't hear her because I left the room and went into my bedroom and lay down on my bed, near the window, under the pine tree. I had felt it, the change in atmosphere, and a kind of thickness settled over me, as if the air were clogged with something making it hard to breathe.

After the letter came in March, they decided to tell me. One night after Burr and the baby had been put to bed and Margie had gone home in the pickup truck with J.D., Walter called me into the kitchen where he sat drinking tea with my mother. My mother said, "We think you're old enough to know what's going on."

Then Walter told me the superintendent had called him into his office a week or so ago to tell him the FBI had been around asking questions about him. Mr. T., the little man whose body had been twisted and bent by polio, walked with one side leaning down and it made him look hunchbacked. When he crossed the playground on his way into our building, kids snickered and called out behind his back, "Here comes the hunchback of Notre Dame." I had never joined in the name calling, and because I knew he liked my stepfather, it had made me uncomfortable, the way it always did when someone got singled out and picked on.

Walter watched my face as he talked. "Mr. T. said he told them I was a good teacher. He said he would ignore them if he could."

"Well," I said, feeling somewhat relieved, "then we can stay here?"

He and my mother exchanged a look. "Now, it seems the FBI has gone to the school board with their lies."

"Everyone likes you," I said. "No one will believe them." But I could feel that old sick feeling in the pit of my stomach.

"I wish it were that simple," said my mother.

"They want you to stay, don't they?"

"Yes," said Walter, "I believe they do, but people believe in the FBI. They think they're beyond reproach, and if they're saying bad things about someone, there must be something to it. At least that's what some of them think. Others are just plain scared of them. The upshot of it is...they sent me a letter telling me they're not going to renew my contract."

I stood still, trying to push away the pain that had come rushing in. "You mean we have to *leave*?"

"There's certainly nothing else to stay for in this God forsaken place," said my mother.

"What about the basketball team?"

"Oh honey." My mother's voice had an edge of exasperation in it.

"You're not even upset," I accused. "You don't even care that everything's ruined."

"Of course I care. This is the best job Walter's had for a while. We need another year to get on our feet. But what can we do?"

She said it like she knew I would get it. But I wasn't giving up so easily this time. "What do they want from you, anyway?"

They exchanged another look. Then my mother said, "Just like in California. They want us to talk to them, to answer their questions."

"Can't you just talk to them?"

Outrage filled my mother's face. "You don't know what you're saying. We can't answer their questions. Our answers might ruin people's lives, people who are guilty of nothing except doing what they believed in, people who were union organizers or who worked for justice for Negroes."

In spite of myself, I remembered the black girl on the corner. My mother studied my face. When she spoke next, her voice was calmer. "Is that what you want--for us to tattle on our friends, so they can be followed around like we are?"

I hesitated, feeling the old guilt flooding in, except this time it didn't quite replace the anger, "I don't know." My voice sounded sulky even to me.

"Well, think about it," she said, some of the indignation back in her voice.

I realized she had expected me to see it their way. But all I wanted was to stay in one place, and drink cherry cokes with my friends. I felt my heart harden. "Maybe if you just talk to them," I said. "They'll see you're not doing anything wrong."

My mother sighed. "It just isn't that simple."

"I'm sick of moving all the time," I said, louder.

"Don't forget we have all of us to consider. It's not exactly a picnic for us either."

There it was again. Everyone thought they had suffered the most. But this time I wasn't going to make it easier for them, not when things were finally going my way, not when I was the Class Queen. I felt the hardness in my heart go deeper. "I'm not leaving," I said.

"Don't be silly," said my mother. But I was already part way out the door.

On Saturday, we were invited to Mr. T.'s house for dinner. We ate fried chicken and mashed potatoes and fresh snap beans and tomato and cucumber salad. His daughter Margo and I were each given a tall glass of milk with ice cubes, and after dinner, we moved into the living room so the adults could talk. Mrs. T. served us chocolate cake on little pink china plates. She passed out pink napkins with the coffee cups.

Margo T. and I mostly sat around listening to the adults. She was in the fifth grade, and we didn't know each other except by sight on the playground. Mrs. T. suggested she take me up to see her bridal doll collection, and we spent an hour or so in her pink and white bedroom while she carefully took each of a dozen or so dolls down from their cupboard and let me examine their frilly dresses and pretty yellow curls. I might have been jealous of Margo's cool brick house and frothy bedroom if it hadn't been for that laughter on the playground.

When we went back downstairs, Mr. T. was leaning his good side toward Walter saying, "You think differently from most people, but I think you're a good man. I don't believe you're what they say you are. I've never heard you say anything dangerous to anyone."

"Of course he hasn't," said my mother.

"They say you're against the government. Is that true?"

Walter took his time answering. I could see him choosing his words carefully. "I'm certainly against this administration; against their crazy witch hunt. But I'm not against government, just ones that are unjust and favor only the guys with money and power."

Mr. T. seemed very small in the big easy chair. His delicate fingers played with the fabric absentmindedly, but his voice was clear when he spoke, "I'm a southerner. I know all about the boys in Washington playing favorites. You're an honest man. That much I know. Your leaving is a loss for us."

"Why'd you have to tell me?" I screamed at my mother at least once every couple of days. "Why'd you have to ruin it for me?"

Sometimes my mother would try to explain again, and sometimes she'd scream back. "Don't be so selfish. Can't you think of anyone but yourself?"

But it didn't matter what she said because every day I walked around on tiptoe, carrying my worry like a hard cherry pit in the bottom of stomach while I waited for some sign that everyone knew. Even when no one acted any differently, I still had such a heavy feeling, I could barely finish my peach cobbler, and even the cherry coke I drank on the way home tasted flat.

I watched for telltale signs: Did my teacher call on me as much? Did she smile at me as often? And I began to find them everywhere, little things mostly, a cross word, an unexpected frown. When Martha Rae said, "Come on slowpoke," I thought, *she wouldn't have said that a month ago.*

I began to look for what *wasn't* done as well. No one paid me as much attention. It could be that they were just used to me by now, or it could be the whispers. "That's how they work," my mother had said, "they let whispers do their dirty work."

Once I came upon Edna Dale and Jo Marie talking together in the hall outside our classroom door. Even in the days when I had been Class Queen, Edna Dale had been the most adored girl in class. But she walked through life unconcerned, acting like being adored was her birthright. I, on the other hand, had alternated between basking in my glory and feeling like I didn't deserve my popularity. Never had I taken it for granted. Now, as I approached them, they turned toward me, the words freezing on their lips, their eyes guilty. I wanted to run, to find another safe corner to hide in, but there were no brick corners on this playground. Here, I was too visible in the bright, sun.

When I went home and told my mother no one liked me anymore, she said, "It's like the end of a marriage when you blow everything out of proportion."

But all I knew was that it felt like the end of everything. I hated her because she could hide out at home with the babies, and I walked the trail of whispers every day.

Grandma brought over my favorite banana cream cake, crinkled up her eyes and wagged her finger at me and said not to worry because "the truth will set you free." But I wanted to be ignorant and rooted.

Walter went around with his quiet face these days. Not that he'd ever been talkative, but this was different. He acted preoccupied, almost as if he were sleepwalking. At school, he went around, smiling a lot, like he'd always done, but at home his silence had a different tone. I noticed it the same way I noticed that my mother lost her temper more often. But we never talked about Walter's silence because we had trouble putting words to what went unspoken and because it scared us in a way my mother's temper never did. Sometimes I'd walk into a room to find him just standing there, his eyes not quite focused, his lips moving silently, like he might be praying.

In May the sixth grade graduated, and everyone got caught up in the fuss. School got out early down here because nearly all the kids helped pick the huge strawberry crops that supported the town. The boys acted more nonchalant about the coming event, but the girls went around in a fever pitch over their dresses and hairdos. I wanted something pink and frilly, but as usual, my mother didn't want me to waste money on a dress I'd never be able to wear any place else. "We've got to put aside every spare cent we can for the move," she reminded me.

But I wasn't going to end up with another grey suit, not down here where it was all pastels and lace. We compromised on a simple white taffeta. Then there was the problem of my hair. I fought with the unruly curls on a daily basis, and my mother tried her best to tame it into submission, setting her mouth and attacking me with the brush, but my hair would not be subdued. We finally managed to flatten it some, and I could only pray it would be a cool day or otherwise my head would be nothing but frizz. "I would have died with joy to have curly hair," my mother said, like she always did, as we stood in front of her bedroom mirror while she yanked at my hair. "I look like Little Orphan Annie," I told her, clenching my teeth against the pain.

"I should think not. You're much prettier; besides she's a fascist along with that stupid Daddy Warbucks."

I knew *fascist* was the worst insult my mother could bestow. But I still identified with Annie, and it was more than curly hair. Her life was filled with terror and calamity while she waited to be rescued.

On graduation day, we had a parent's party. I waited nervously for my mother to arrive, still worried about what she'd turn up wearing and how late she'd be. I had left her at home, cross and teary, having a bad day. I hoped she didn't forget, or come as late as she did to other school functions. Often she got there way after things had started, all cheery smiles, trying to make up for her lateness with charm.

Just as they served the punch, Martha Ray poked me, and I looked up and there she was. She stood over by the door, looking shy and beautiful in a soft grey dress and black pumps, her dark hair shiny and smooth, a dark rose among the dogwood. She caught my eye and winked. Suddenly, I felt proud of her, and at the same time, an amazing thought flashed across my mind. I wanted my mother to meet Edna Dale. I wanted them to talk, to act like they had always known each other, to make me believe nothing was wrong, and I could go on being the Class Queen forever. Wanting it so badly, willing even to risk rejection and humiliation, I went over to where Edna Dale stood surrounded by her fans and tapped her on the shoulder. "Edna Dale," I said, "I want you to come and meet my mother." Then I held my breath. But Edna Dale just smiled sweetly and took my hand, and I led her over to where my mother stood.

Edna didn't seem at all surprised to be suddenly included in my family, and maybe she was flattered at meeting the principal's wife. After all, he was still the principal, even if he'd been called a "dangerous man." She came with me, her hand docile in mine. I floated up to my mother and said, "Mother, I want you to meet Edna Dale." Then I stepped back a little to better view this historic moment.

Edna stood there serene in white ruffles, her brown hair curled softly on her cheek, her skin the color of fresh peaches. My mother smiled and said,

"It's nice to meet you Edna Dale. That's a very pretty dress you're wearing."

Edna Dale smiled her sweet smile, her I-am-part-of-the gracious-South smile. "Why thank you, Mrs. Miller. I am right pleased to meet you too. We just think the world of Mr. Miller."

I saw the "we" register in my mother's eyes as if Edna Dale spoke for the whole South, but her composure remained unruffled. No matter how bad it got later on, I would remember this moment when it was just like I had pictured it would be. My mother was the Perfect Mother of my fantasies and Edna Dale was still Edna Dale, and I was still holding her hand.

On his birthday late in May, Walter packed the car to head back to the Midwest to look for work. We all stood around in the yard outside my grandparent's cabin where we had moved as soon as school ended. Already the sun burned through the tin roof, and it felt more like August in the crowded cabin with the cook stove blazing to make formula for Lulu. Once again my grandparents had shifted everything around to make room, and once again we brought the pieces of our lives to them. This time, I felt the full weight of our reacquired poverty. This time I wondered if what had been shattered, could ever be made whole again.

We stood huddled together watching him put the last of his things into our old car. My mother stunned into silence, her eyes moving around nervously as she shifted the baby from shoulder to shoulder. Walter, calm as always, moved carefully around the yard, but I could tell by the set of his mouth, he felt bad. Even though not much had passed between Walter and me since the day I found out he wasn't being hired back, now that he was going away, I felt the old heaviness creeping into my arms and legs. I had just begun to accept him as a permanent fixture, almost like a real father, and now he was leaving us.

"I'll find some kind of work right away. It's home, and someone will know where to look," he smiled reassuringly at my mother, who shifted the baby again and bit her bottom lip. Then she smiled bravely, I thought. Just where was this mystical "home" I wondered? Back in Chicago? California? They seemed a million miles away from here. "I'm depending on you to keep those letters coming," Walter said, looking at me, serious, like he really needed something from me.

"Yeah," I said. "Sure." He had given us his aunt's address in Milwaukee, Wisconsin where he could be reached until he settled somewhere. But still, he seemed to be moving off into oblivion, into empty space.

Then he got into the car, backed slowly out of the yard onto the gravel road and drove off into nowhere while we stood there like some family in a magazine reunion, even my mother was waving and smiling, especially Burr, who didn't get it, and kept jumping up and down and laughing because he thought the whole thing was a lot of fun. The baby was the only one of us not smiling. She gazed out from under her sun bonnet, her little face solemn watching Walter's face, the only one of us not trying to make him feel better.

The next morning I struggled out of sleep to the sound of scratching on the screened window above my cot in the kitchen. I opened my eyes and saw Brenda Owens's face pressed against the screen. Even through wire mesh, her eyes twinkled at me. "Christine," she whispered, "C'mon git up, lazy bones. If we hurry we can git to the crik before the heat catches us."

"What time is it?" I asked still groggy with sweaty sleep.

"It's after seven. I'd a been here earlier but I had to finish milking first." She chuckled.

I saw her clearly then, saw her freckled face, the brown eyes watching me in the early morning almost-coolness. She had just milked three cows, and then walked a mile and a half up the dusty road to fetch me. Suddenly the whispers faded; the school year melted away, and it was just like it had been that first day in our front yard, me feeling the solidness of her as she knelt there outside my window, waiting.

"Hey, Brenda," I said. "Did you bring some peanuts?"

If the Owens's had heard about what happened to us, they didn't let on. My friendship with Brenda resumed as if there had never been a Mansfield school, as if I had never been the Class Queen. All summer, I'd get on my bike and ride the mile down hill to the Owens's, so I could follow them around while they did their chores. I'd never actually seen kids work before. My family never expected any regular work from me. Occasionally, my mother asked me to do something, usually when she was desperate and yelling, but nine year old Rhonda and eleven year old Brenda worked in the kitchen garden, did housework and fed and milked three cows apiece every morning and evening. I even stood in cow manure and watched them. It looked easy, but when I tried it, I couldn't get any milk at all. I felt strange grabbing the cow in such a delicate place, afraid I might hurt her, so I squeezed gently, trying at the same time to pull down like I'd seen Brenda do. After a minute, Brenda said she guessed I didn't have the right rhythm. But she sure did. She could talk a mile a minute, chew gum and milk the cow at the same time. When the cow started to pee and some of it splashed into the bucket, I couldn't help making a face, and she said, "A little cow pee never hurt no one. You sure do worry about the funniest things." But her grin took away any sting in her words. Brenda Owens, I thought, had never said a mean thing in her whole life.

But just the same, I refused to drink any of that milk just like I refused to drink water from the dipper because everyone drank from that dipper, and I pictured the lip of it slick with spit and crawling with germs. I was pretty thirsty by the time they invited me to stay for "dinner" as they called it, served at the stroke of noon on a wooden kitchen table. But when they passed the milk pitcher to me, I said, "No, thank you," and then I looked around the table. But no one was paying any attention to me. I was a bit anxious about hurting their feelings and chasing away my only friend. But it was just like Grandpa later said, "They have too much work and worry to think about whether a skinny kid from the North drinks her milk."

While I was dipping my corn bread into my black eyes peas like I'd watched Brenda do, they asked me questions about "up North." J.D., age sixteen, said he'd heard that instead of water, beer ran right out of the faucets in Milwaukee.

I didn't know just what I should tell them. I didn't want to make the same mistake I had made in Denver and get labeled a know-it-all, so I ate a spoonful of black eyed peas, and merely said that beer didn't *exactly* run out of the faucets.

But J.D. was enjoying his story too much to let anything I said get in the way. "Yes siree," he said in between mouthfuls of corn bread, "Billy Conway went up there once and got drunk near about every night."

"I declare," said his mother. His father didn't say a word. A tall, gaunt man, Jeff Owens worked and ate, and he must have slept, but the only one I ever saw him talk with was my grandfather. He acted as if women and children didn't exist, like we were all set pieces at his dinner table. The only words he spoke came at the end of the meal when he'd rise, grab his hat from a peg on the wall, and say, "Chores are waitin" and go back out doors.

"Yep." said J.D., grinning madly, "Billy Conway said it pret near killed him, but he didn't have no choice because the beer just flowed out of them faucets."

Later as I followed them back out toward the barn, Brenda whispered to me that Billy Conway was an "outright fool." But she'd never think of contradicting J.D. to his face. People here didn't scream at each other at the dinner table like we did at home.

"Soon as I'm out of high school," she confided, "I'm going up North and get a job with the FBI."

"The *FBI?*" I was aghast.

But she thought I was just impressed, and she smiled and said, "Yep. Margie's gettin' married in May and they're movin' to Washington D.C. because Bill has a job with the FBI. It's so excitin'. They promised to get me in. Yaw'll see. I'll do it."

I shuddered thinking about Brenda as an FBI agent, looking us up in their files, maybe even sent to track us down. I looked down at her cheeks, rosy under her freckles while I tried to picture her in a trench coat, her eyes hard as daggers. "It's not all it's cracked up to be," I told her. Usually Brenda listened to me, the voice of authority about most everything outside of Arkansas, but now she just narrowed her eyes and studied my face.

When I finally staggered home on Sunday, all the way up hill with the sun beating down on my head, weak from hunger and parched from thirst, I was dying to tell them about Brenda. While my mother sat at the table with me and fed the baby, I drank a quart of store milk and gobbled a whole bowl of strawberries, and then I told them about Brenda joining the FBI. Grandma sat at one end of the table shelling peas while Grandpa lay on the couch against the wall taking his mid-day rest. "She's still young," my grandmother said. "She'll change her mind."

"I don't think so. You don't know Brenda when she makes up her mind about something." I was seeing her freckles dark against her pale skin the night she told me she hadn't eaten in three days because she wanted to be skinny for Margie's wedding.

My mother frowned. Then Grandma said, "That Pebble is a marvel. The other day she said, 'Mrs. Christie, I'm right pleased that Margie's gittin' out of here. I want my girls to have it easier'n it's been for me.'"

"Well, her girls are gonna turn us in," I said.

""Her mind's been poisoned already," said my mother."Maybe you should stay away from there."

That scared me. "But she's the only friend I've got left," I said.

"Well, read a good book." It was what she always said.

Grandpa cleared his throat, and I thought he was going to tease me about marrying J.D. and having a passel of snot noses like he usually did., but instead he said, "You'd want to be an FBI agent too or any damn thing that might get you out of a lifetime spent scratching in that red dirt trying to get something to grow. Jeff Owens works from sun up to sun down, and he still barely ekes out enough to feed his kids. You bet they're tickled pink to get away from here." He said all this with his eyes closed without moving the cold rag lying across his forehead.

I didn't get it. I couldn't believe Grandpa would defend her for going over to the enemy side, and now he made it sound like being here really was awful. All the time I had thought he at least liked it here, loved the melons and Jackson and the trees he was always saying would make us all rich someday. Now, he sounded just as miserable as my mother and grandmother. I didn't know which hurt worse--the thought that Brenda might turn into the enemy one day, or that Grandpa might have fooled me about liking it here so much.

Later on, still feeling uneasy, I wandered out to the pasture in back of the house where Grandpa stood by the wood fence hovering over Bessie, the big brown and white cow, the one I always imitated when she wandered up by the fence. Grandpa looked up, saw me and grinned. Then I noticed something wet and slimy slowly emerging from Bessie's broad rump. "Watch her now," said Grandpa, "her young un's about to be born." Bessie, her head bent toward the ground, seemed unconcerned as she continued nibbling grass. Every now and then she mooed, a low, drawn out sound. "Does it hurt?" I asked Grandpa.

"Of course it does. Don't you hear her?"

But I couldn't associate those cow sounds with pain, and if it did hurt, I didn't understand how she could just go on calmly munching grass even as the calf was sliding clear, guided by grandpa who smiled and murmured comforting sounds, reaching up now and then to pat her broad rump, more involved it seemed than the mother. "That's the way cows are," said Grandpa, "Mother cows don't worry themselves into a frazzle the way humans do."

Then I got caught up in watching the calf emerge inch by inch until finally, it slid out into grandpa's waiting hands and then lay struggling in a pile of damp ooze on the grass. Grandpa looked straight at me and nodded, a gesture of wonderment, his smile was a chuckle of sheer happiness. "Hey Dolly," he called, "What do you think about that? She's something, hey?"

"Oh Grandpa," I said, leaning forward with my chest pressed hard against the fence, my arms reaching towards them, forgetting I had ever doubted him. "She's just... wonderful."

Early in July they brought the goat tied up in the back of a pick-up truck. I had been reading on the porch, and I could hear her bleating even before they pulled into the yard. Feeling slow and heavy with heat, I went outside in time to see Grandpa go around to the back of the truck, let down the back gate and pull her down into the yard. I could see she was scared, the way she pulled against the rope and kind of pranced back from him on her tiny hooves.

"Come on, you stinking old flea bag," he said. I didn't pay any attention. It was just his way of talking to his animals. Then I remembered they said they were going to get a goat to supply my sister and brother with milk. Grandpa led the goat to a pen in a corner of the pasture where Jackson and I took walks together, and I followed. Maybe it was that baby calf I had seen being born that gave me the courage to ask him. "Can I milk her?"

He looked at me thoughtfully a moment. "You gotta have strong hands," he said.

"I do," I promised.

He smiled in a way I could tell he didn't believe me. "Do you want to get up at 6:00 a.m. every day?" he asked.

I thought about how my mother always said he'd never teach his kids anything about farming, so I swallowed and said, "I don't care."

"Tell you what," he said, "if your hands are strong enough to get any milk out of her, I'll do the morning milking and you the night."

The next day at 6:00 P.M. we went out to her shed together. Grandma had suggested I might want to stay in and learn to wash dishes instead. But I wanted real chores like the Owens's had, not girlish ones like dishes. Still, I felt nervous like I did before a test in school, and it didn't help any that Grandpa didn't say a word until he had put down the bucket, pulled up a stool and sat down. "Look here," he said, "watch what I do." And he began to pull down hard on her long teats in a rhythm like I had seen Brenda and her sister use on the cows. Milk began to come down in streams into the bucket. "Goats are tough to milk," he said. "Grown women can't always get the milk to come down." I knew he was saying that because he expected I'd fail. After a few moments, he stopped milking her and stood up.

When I sat down on the stool, the goat turned her head and looked at me, and I reached over and patted her neck. Then I took a deep breath and grabbed a hold of her teats like Grandpa had done. They felt dry and soft like talcum powder in the palm of my hand. I squeezed gently, so I wouldn't hurt her and pulled at the same time. Nothing happened.

"Grab a hold, Dolly," Grandpa said.

So I pulled harder and then harder, and I began to get a rhythm going, and then I heard the first milk begin to splash against the metal bucket. I turned and grinned at Grandpa, and he grinned and shook his head like he did when he was tickled. "Atta girl," he said. "You'll be a farmer yet."

I got so I could milk her faster than he could because it seemed she liked me better and let down her milk better for me, after all. He pretended to gripe about it, but I could tell he was really proud of the way I handled her. He began to trust me with her, and I started taking her for walks, leading her by a rope around the pasture. "Don't ever let go of that rope," Grandpa warned me the first time. "Goats are stupid, and she'll run herself into the fence or out into the woods and get herself lost. So hang on tight!"

One day I was bringing her back to her shed when I saw Grandpa walking toward the barn. I yelled to him because I wanted him to see how nice she walked with me. But the sudden noise must have startled Nanny. The next thing I knew she had jerked the rope, knocking me off my feet, and suddenly I was being pulled across the field on my stomach. I grabbed the rope with both hands, holding on for dear life. Grandpa had turned at the sound of my voice, and now I saw him start toward us, calling out, moving more quickly than I had known he could, moving up and over the fence. Fear had given Nanny strength, and she plowed on heading straight for the woodpile. I held on tight although I could feel the ground scraping right through my shirt, afraid now that she would dash us both against the logs.

"Let go! For God's sake," Grandpa called, and finally his screams penetrated, and I dropped the rope a few feet from the woodpile. When I let go, Nanny stopped in her tracks.

I lay there on the rough ground, feeling too dizzy to get up, my heart pounding. I felt him squat down beside me, and I twisted my head toward him."You told me not to let go," I said, not accusingly, just reminding him.

Our eyes met. Then he put his huge hand on my hair, gently, and shook his head, and for an incredible moment I thought he might be going to cry.

Every Saturday my grandparents went into town to do their shopping. Last summer, I had always gone in with them. While Grandpa talked crops with the men, Grandma talked to everyone. It was just like Grandpa always said, "Leave her alone five minutes and she tells her life story." A lot of times she listened, saying things like "Goodness me," while some lady from the feed store stood there telling her every detail of her husband's dinner right down to the way he liked his gravy fixed with milk. At first, I had thought she was only pretending to be interested, but anyone could look at her eyes all lit up and sparkly and know she actually liked this talk.

By midsummer, I began to feel something sullen in the air, making me stutter again when I tried to talk. Even just saying "Good Mornin'" was enough to make my tongue go thick. And once when my mother and I were in town without my grandparents, I saw Mrs. Barns come toward us, look up, see us and then deliberately cross the street.

Earlier this summer I had asked my grandmother why we should go in to town at all if everyone was going to hate us so much.

"We need groceries is why," said Grandpa.

"Besides," added my grandmother, "people don't hate us, and what of it if they did? Remember you're good as the best and better'n the rest." She continued to wave and smile at everyone.

One time I saw Jeff Owens leaning up against the wall outside the general store, his thumbs hooked into the suspenders holding up his jeans. He tipped his hat and smiled back at us, his face breaking into about a million tiny lines, his face, homely as ever, was suddenly right as rain.

"Sure is a hot one," he called through the snuff he kept tucked inside his lower lip.

I was in town with my grandparents the day I ran into Martha Raye in the back of the drugstore where we had sipped cherry cokes and giggled over movie magazines back in March, a million years ago. She stood with her mother and her cousin George. Then Martha saw me, and her face lit up. I was so glad to see her I could hardly stand it, wanting to know everything that had happpened to my friends since we moved to the farm. She came over and took my hand. "Are y'all having a good summer?" she asked.

I hesitated a second before I said, "So-so. How about you?"

"Oh Christine," she said, "My cousin George is here for the summer. Just think!"

I had met George once or twice when he came to visit, and I knew Martha Ray adored him. I smiled to see her so warm and excited like in the old days when we walked around arm in arm and told each other everything.

Then George noticed us, and he called out. "Hey."

Martha Ray, still hanging on to my hand turned toward her cousin. "Look George. It's Christine. Wasn't I just telling you about our great games?"

George smiled a mean little smile. Then he said, "Hey Christine. I hear your daddy's a Red."

The smile faded on Martha Ray's face, went out like someone blowing out a match. I felt my stomach drop. I knew I should defend Walter, but I couldn't think what to say. I just stood there feeling shame crawling up my neck, as if George might be right, and there really was something wrong about us. Then Martha Raye's mother turned and saw us. I saw her lips press together and before I could even manage "Hello, Mrs. Raye," she had pulled Martha by the arm and marched her toward the door. This was the same woman who had kissed me goodnight so tenderly while my sister was being born, who had baked gooey cookies and then worried about our cavities, the woman who was my Perfect Mother. I stood rooted to the spot. Everything around me had gone still. In the background I could hear the murmur of the druggist's voice a long way off. There was a faint buzzing coming from the clock on the back wall, and a huge horsefly landed on the display of hairspray near my arm. All of this seemed to be happening in a film, a story about someone else. I watched Martha Raye turn before they went through the door and our eyes met. Hers were sad and maybe a little scared. Then they were gone. I felt my heart drop, leaving a hole in my chest, burning in the afternoon heat.

I never saw Martha Raye again. But sometimes lying on the front porch that summer, tired of reading, my little sister playing next to me on a blanket, her face would just sort of pop into my head and hang there in the air like the Cheshire cat. I wrote her imaginary letters, and she answered them with pledges of her undying love, telling me how much she missed me. I tried never to think about her mother because whenever I saw those lips pressed together, those cold eyes, I felt weak inside like I might never lift my head from the porch chair, not even to pick up my sister's toy, or go into the house for lunch, like I might have to lie on the cement porch floor forever, too tired even to care.

The days stretched out forever, long and hot, broken only by my walks with Nanny, and swatting flies off Jackson, each day as unchanging as the day before, so dry the road turned into dust clouds and the ground felt hard as bricks. Increasingly, as the summer dragged on, the days seemed to build toward anger until it surged through the tiny cabin, like sudden bolts of electricity. It had been hard enough being crowded together the summer before when we still had the year ahead, when the cabin had seemed only a brief moment in our lives. Now, it felt like time had stopped. Trapped together in the heat that held us like a vise, my mother and grandmother, their faces red and frazzled in the unbearable kitchen, began their mornings in a kind of daze as they pushed against the heat, their movements jerky, like string dolls, their voices rising over the crackle of wood in the cook stove.

"Here now. Let go. The damn thing's not hot enough yet."

"It's hot enough in here to kill a person. Oh God! Maybe he'll just disappear in the bowels of Milwaukee."

"Stop that kind of talk! He's a good man."

"Good men have been known to desert a sinking ship."

"Shh. The kids'll hear you."

"I don't give a damn who hears me!"

Even if I moved out onto the porch, their voices found me, my mother's growing louder, the language stronger, my grandmother getting wilder. No matter where I stood, I could see grandma's grey hair sticking out in wisps around her red cheeks, her eyes dark. "Spoiled brats, all of you, ungrateful for what God's given you."

"What's to be grateful for? Nothing but unending work surrounded by a sea of ignorance."

"You have three beautiful children and a good man."

"A missing one."

"Don't even think such a thing!

"What makes you so damn sure he's coming back?"

"Because he's not the kind of man to leave his family. Shame on you!"

"If I were he, maybe I wouldn't come back either, once I'd escaped this Hellhole!"

I went out of the house then, out to the pasture where Grandpa had taken Jackson for his daily exercise. But I kept hearing my mother's words anyway, and they made my stomach tighten. A missing man. Another missing father. It made me angry at her because she had married him and now he was part of my family, and if I couldn't trust them, then who could I trust? Not my friends. Martha Ray had proven that. If only my real father were here, I thought, he would know what to do. He'd get us out of here, take us some place where they'd never find us, where we'd have a house and a yard and horses. I looked out past the pasture, out passed the tall pines, dark against the sky. I pictured my father coming across the field, riding fast on his Palomino. I could hear the hoof beats as he rode faster, coming to rescue me. But when I looked in the direction of the sound, I saw it was only the preacher's old car pulling into our yard.

Usually, the preacher arrived in the early afternoon on Sunday. Now that I stayed home on Sunday morning because I didn't feel up to facing anyone at church, I read away the morning on the porch with my mother, digging into the box of books Walter had left behind, both of us quiet, suffering from the same kind of sleeping sickness.

Even in the heat, when my grandparents came back from church, Grandma would go take off her good dress and the ruby brooch Aunt Bee left her, put on a house dress and a clean apron and go out and stoke up the stove for a pie. If there was a pie in the cook stove, the preacher'd stop for sure.

When the preacher came, he kind of skipped up to the porch, his little eyes already feverish, darting around, his nose quivering like he smelled sin. The preacher stuck his nose through the door saying, "Evenin' to y'all. The Lord sure is lookin' down with pleasure on us today."

Grandpa, across the porch in his rocker, leaned over and spit into his can. "Mornin' Bill, " he said, "If you'd been out pickin' bugs off your melon like I've been, you wouldn't think it's so God damned fine out there." He always looked up in time to enjoy the way the preacher winced at the name of the Lord taken in vain.

My grandmother came out and said, "Why Gosh sakes, come on in." She always acted surprised and pleased to see them. She laughed in her merry, company way and said, "There's a pie."

The preacher smiled at my grandmother, a slow almost sleepy smile, and I saw my grandmother go red right up into her hair. I hated the way he made my grandmother blush and laugh. Whenever his eyes settled momentarily on me, I felt squirmy.

The preacher's wife followed him in, her dull, thin brown hair tightly curled around her head, her fat cheeks creased into a perpetual smile framing the largest teeth I had ever seen. They protruded slightly, and because she smiled all of the time, they sort of took over her face.

"While you're at it," Grandpa went on calmly, "why don't you ask that God of yours for some water? My melon sure would appreciate it."

"I was just saying," said my grandmother, "that we hadn't had a visit from you folks for a while now, wasn't I, Daddy dear?"

My grandfather leaned down and spat a long stream into his can. "Sit, for gosh sakes." My grandmother motioned them into a couple of wooden kitchen chairs.

The preacher's wife, who had been smiling the whole time, settled herself onto the chair, carefully folding her skirt underneath and kind of scrunching around on the seat like she might be testing it for bumps. Then she giggled. I had once heard my grandfather say that one day "when that woman sits herself down on my porch, silent as a cow and giggles at me with that mouth full of teeth, I swear to their God, I'm going to wrap my hands around her fat neck and strangle her then and there."

Occasionally, the preacher's wife would lean over to offer my grandmother a tidbit of gossip, like a piece of candy. Mostly though, she sat and fanned herself with a church pamphlet, smiled and giggled. Especially she giggled whenever my grandfather's voice rose in anger over something the preacher said. The preacher never stopped trying to convert my grandfather.

"You'd think the fool would have enough brains to know he can't change the way I think," my grandfather would say after they had picked themselves up and sidled off the porch. "Imagine him having gall enough to believe a little weasel like him could change my mind about a thing!"

Sometimes they brought their skinny daughter Mary Ann with them. Mary Ann had hair the color of oleo before Grandma mixed in the yellow and pale skin that never seemed to see any sun. She kept as silent as her mother until Grandma shooed us off the porch. Then we'd go outside and stand around still not saying much until finally, Mary Ann would pat her shirt and say, "Let's go to the barn and I'll show you somethin'." Then we'd go out to the barn and sit in the hay while she pulled out her latest True Romance magazine. I was truly amazed and a little embarrassed by them. I couldn't equate the pictures I saw of men and women groping at each other with the version of sexual intercourse told to me by my mother.

But Mary Ann turned the pages lazily, "Did you ever think about your parents *doing* it?"

I never had and I wasn't sure I wanted to now. "I don't think they do," I said, shifting uncomfortably in the prickly hay.

Luann caressed the pages. "Course they do," she said. "Don't *you* ever wonder about it? About doing it?"

"No," I said. "We're too young."

"I know someone who's done it, and she's only 12." Her eyes were dreamy. "I think about it, what it's like and all."

"Ask your parents," I told her helpfully. "They must know about it."

Luann looked at me, incredulous. Then she giggled. For a moment I heard the ghost of her mother's silly laugh. "Don't be silly. My daddy's a preacher," she said smiling, her eyes clouding over again, like her mind was somewhere else.

One Sunday, they invited me over to their house for Sunday "dinner." I went, even though my mother and grandfather shook their heads in disapproval because boredom had driven me to do just about anything to break the monotony of my days. The preacher's family lived in a square box, bare around the outside without even a tree to break up the hard ground or to keep the sun from pounding the roof. Even so, I could see right off they were a lot better off than the Owens's.

We ate in their spotless kitchen at a Formica topped table which was set with blue and white dishes that had pictures of people from colonial days and tall glasses filled with bluish milk. We ate fried chicken, corn that had been scraped off the cob, biscuits and gravy and mashed potatoes that came to the table in a cut glass bowl with a design swirled into the top. I couldn't get over how quiet everything was and how orderly. Each part of the meal had its place and everyone seemed to know what to expect next, unlike my own household where the unexpected always waited.

We all sat down at the table except for the preacher's wife who brought in a plate of fried chicken, smiling as she set it on the table, making her cooing sounds. She wore a large cotton apron over her beige linen church dress. Next, she placed the bowl of potatoes tenderly, even lovingly on the table in front of us. No one said, "Oh, for God's sake sit down," like my mother did when grandma tried to serve us. We all sat there waiting while the food smells filled the kitchen making my mouth water. But I was afraid to move. It was almost like being in church. Then the preacher's wife took off her apron, folded it carefully over the back of her chair and sat down, a signal for the preacher to bow his head for the prayer. It was a long prayer, and I fidgeted a bit, but I kept my head bowed and my eyes closed till I heard him say "Amen."

Then the preacher's wife passed the platter of fried chicken to the preacher first. He carefully lifted a drumstick from the plate, took a small bite and said, "Chicken's overcooked." And the preacher's wife smiled and passed the potatoes which tasted salty and watery, bone white, as if some of the taste had been bleached out. I knew better than to expect loud talk about the fate of the working class in Cold War America, but I expected we'd talk about something, church, even. But nobody said a word, and nobody pushed all his food together into a pie and then cut it into wedges either. They all just spooned the food into their mouths and Luann kept her head down over her plate. Once, the preacher looked at me with his creepy, little round eyes and asked me how my grandfather was feeling, like he'd been sick or something.

"Just fine," I said brightly.

The preacher nodded solemnly and muttered something about "the wages of sin." I knew from listening to them that the preacher thought my grandfather must be weighed down by all the "sin" he carried around inside him.

Once, the preacher's wife smiled vaguely in my direction and said, "Drink your milk, honey, before it gets warm." I looked at the huge glass of bluish milk that still had about a half dozen ice cubes floating in it and wondered how I could possibly choke it all down. Finally, the preacher rose, scraped back his chair, and as if on some kind of family cue, everyone else rose too, and Lu Ann and I escaped outside to read romance magazines on the straggly grass parched brown by the afternoon sun.

On the days the preacher and his wife came to visit, my grandparents often had a fight after they left. It could start over any little thing, and suddenly they went galloping back into the past.

"You're just like your father," my grandmother often told him on these hot afternoons

"You'll never let it go, will you," roared my grandfather back. "You'll hound a man to his grave! God damn you anyway!"

Sometimes I was smart enough to get up from the porch chair where I had been sunk in a stupor all afternoon and go outside where I couldn't hear them. I knew my grandfather would be sitting on the couch, one boot off and dangling from his hand, with his pant leg rolled up, rubbing his bad leg. "You're a ridiculous old woman," he'd say.

Sometimes my mother got involved."Dad! Stop it!" I could hear her yelling no matter where I was, her voice carried even out to the yard."You two have been doing this my whole life," she said. "And it never changes; you never solve a thing."

Grandma would be crying now, and soon Grandpa would bang out of the door, clamping his hat on his head as he went.

"Why are they fighting?" I asked her once.

"Who knows?" my mother said, disgust in her voice. "Something sets them off, the heat, anything, and once they get started they can go back fifty years and bring it all back up. They're both a couple of old fools," she said and began clearing the table.

"I'm sick of this place," I said, "Walter better send for us quick."

"Maybe he has no intention of sending for us," she said, calmly picking up the dishes."

A belt of fear closed around my stomach. "Don't say that!" I told her sharply.

"Well, it's probably true. Why would he want a wife and three kids to weigh him down now?"

My voice sputtered. "But you guys always said we could depend on our family even *if all else failed* you used to say. Now, you've forgotten that?"

My mother stood there, her face averted, the skin around her eyes looked bruised. Then she turned abruptly went into the bedroom.

I waited a moment to see if she would come back, listening to the sounds of dishes in the kitchen. A mud dobber buzzed merrily around its clay house in the corner of the living room right under where grandpa took his afternoon naps. Then I went out into the yard, heading for the barn without really thinking about it. They've all gone crazy, I thought. I could see Grandpa way out at the end of the field, bent over his melon. I went into the barn, into the cool darkness where Jackson stood in his stall munching hay and took the fly swatter down from its hook next to his stall. He snorted when he saw me, glad to see me, I thought, while I scattered the flies, smelling the sweet/sour hay odor and listening to Jackson chewing.

I remembered the story my uncle told back in California about how after one of their fights, my grandfather would bring a rope to the barn and say hc was going to hang himself. Maybe all the fighting had worn him down. Maybe he couldn't stand it anymore either. And that scared me most of all because if Grandpa cracked, the one I thought would never be afraid of anything, the one who had chased the Bully Boys out of Michigan, the one who had thrown a grown man over his barbed wire fence, if he couldn't stand it, then I didn't see how I could. I let my eyes roam around the stall, but I didn't see any sign of a rope.

That night when Grandpa came into supper, he did a strange thing. Instead of sitting down at the kitchen table, he lay down on the bed in the kitchen and turned his face to the wall, covering his eyes with one arm. Grandma moved around the kitchen silently getting supper. I stood in the doorway and watched them, but they both ignored me. Grandpa looked old lying there during supper time when he should be reading the newspaper or trading stories with my mother, lying there with his work boots dangling off the edge, not touching the clean spread.

I could see Grandma moving back and forth, beginning to set dishes on the table. "Soup's on," she said like she always did, but she wasn't smiling tonight or teasing me, or even reminding me to "wash off all those nasty microbes."

My mother came in from the bedroom with the baby draped across her shoulder. She came up beside me in the doorway and looked down at her father and shook her head."Why don't you, two, give it up," she said.

"Mind your own beeswax," said Grandma, going past her with a dish of strawberries. We ate them on everything since we had a bumper crop and Grandma said it was sinful to waste food with all those "poor children still starving over in Europe." She'd been saying that for years like we had so much to waste. It seemed to me we were the ones who were poor, eating most of our meals from the garden and scraping up cash to go into town for margarine or toilet paper because, my mother said, she refused to use the catalogue pages like they used to back in Michigan.

"Look," said my mother now, absently patting the baby as she talked, "Admit it. You can't live with each other, but you certainly can't live without each other. Look at him. Just lying there helpless as a calf."

Like a magic word had been spoken, my grandfather pulled back his arm and turned his head toward my grandmother standing by the stove. "Silly, old woman," his words soft this time, a caress.

"Time to eat, daddy," she said, still not looking at him, but her voice lower too.

My mother shook her head wonderingly, and rolled her eyes up toward the ceiling. "Couple of old fools," she said.

And I, wanting the unbearable summer to end, afraid Walter really might not send for us, feeling like I'd die if I had to stay here another minute, much less another month, would sit down with them at the table and pass the strawberries, washed and shiny in the glass bowl and long for cobbler, knowing full well that I would never feel that sweet biscuit dough in my mouth again.

One day, a day just as unbearable and boring as the day before, I was reading out on the porch, next to my baby sister, lying in her buggy while the air shimmered around us. My mother came out of the house, stopping to bend over the baby and to dab her cheeks, pink with heat rash, with a cool cloth. I glanced over at her and then went back to my book, both of us too hot to talk. She went out the screen door and into the yard. I knew she must be going out to the road to check on the mail. Earlier in the summer, I, too, used to wait expectantly for the mail to come, hoping for the letter that would tell us we were free at last. But I had stopped waiting, had stopped, I believed, even caring. It was easier, I was learning, not to care, not to get your hopes up only to have then dashed by cold eyes or the neglect of a missing father.

Something made me look up from my book and out through the screen door to see my mother's head bent over some mail in her hand. Then I saw her wave what looked like a letter in the air. I got up and opened the screen door, and my mother started to run toward me. Even from across the yard, I could see her excitement. I met her halfway, and she twirled me around, laughing, dancing me around like she used to when I had been barely up to her waist. Now we were eye to eye. "Hallelujah! We're on our way," she yelled. She kept kissing me and laughing. "Chicago, Chicago that toddling town, that toddling town..." she sang while the world spun around us.

Turned out, once again, we weren't going to Chicago. Instead, we were going to a strange city called Milwaukee, the city where Walter had grown up, a city where he still had relatives and where he had landed a job. I knew it was near Chicago, and I'd worry about getting there later. For right now, just getting away from heat and hatred was good enough. "Come with us!" I pleaded with my grandmother. "It'll be our old life again!"

But Grandma smiled down at me like she knew something I didn't. "Please!" I can't go without you."

"Nonsense. Can't never did anything," she said.

A few days later, I tried working on Grandpa. "Can't leave," he said, "who'll swat flies off Jackson?"

"He can come too," I said, even though I knew that was impossible.

Grandpa just sat there on the sofa with his pants leg rolled up rubbing his bad leg. Then I did something I had never done before. I sat down next to him and kissed his scratchy cheek. He looked startled, but then his eyes smiled, and he nodded approvingly at me. "Aghh Dolly," he said, "your grandpa's an old man." I didn't answer, just sat gingerly on the edge of the sofa, watching him, while he rubbed his leg.

When he spoke again, his voice had more energy. "You should have seen me when I was young and stood 6'2"." He grinned down at me. "My brother Joe and I used to sneak my dad's whiskey, then go to town and raise Hell. There wasn't a man in the county who could stand up to me." He let go of his pants leg, and leaned forward, gazing down at his arms propped on his thighs, opening and closing his huge, gnarled hands, turning them into fists, and gazing down at them. "Now these hands are stiff as my pump handle. Stiff and rusty with the rheumatism." He laughed, snorted really, a sound without much humor and shook his head. He looked over at me while I sat waiting as if I knew I'd never again sit with my grandfather while he spun these tales of his. "You know, I had to leave engineering school," he went on, "to go back to that damn rocky Michigan land because my folks needed me. Dad couldn't keep it going anymore.

Then later, Mocky and I moving from farm to farm until that last one, Cook's Place--the one that should have been ours forever, the one the banks stole out from under me." He shook his head ruefully, the way he always did. "And losing those baby boys and then your Aunt Bee..." He paused, still looking down at his hands. "Every time I thought about your daddy..." He turned then and searched my face. "Without my anger, I'd never be able to get out of bed in the morning, to drag these old bones out there. Anger gives me the strength to work, to breathe." Then he rolled down his pants leg, picked himself up off the chair, winking at me like he always did when he got serious, to take the edge off, took down his old hat with the sweat stain around the brim and went out to stand by the side of the road like he did every afternoon.

Later, I'd see him in my mind's eye standing alongside that dusty road in the early evening heat with watermelon as long as a man's arm and musk melon big as pumpkins piled beside him on the gravel. He said the fruit belonged to his neighbors as much as it did to him who had watered it and picked bugs off its leaves with his clumsy fingers. "Theirs," he said, "because we share the same earth." He'd hail them down as they came back from Saturday shopping, and the red dirt farmers would stop their rattling trucks, take the fruit he held out to them and with a quick, "Thankee," drive off down the road looking more than a little bewildered by the old man standing in the unbearable sun with a rag tied around his head to soak up the sweat.

March 9, 1954

[Fred] Friendly and [Edward R.] Murrow collected film of the senator's speeches and his committee hearings of his television appearances and news interviews. They gathered parts of these into a half-hour documentary so that the senator's methods of bullying witnesses and opponents were obvious to the viewers.

Viewers saw McCarthy condemn himself out of his own mouth. At the end of the program Murrow said:

"We will not walk in fear of one another...We are not descended from fearful men, not from men who feared to write, to speak, to associate and to defend causes that were for the moment unpopular. This is no time...to keep silent...

We proclaim ourselves, as indeed we are, the defenders of freedom—what's left of it—but we cannot defend freedom abroad by deserting it at home."

There was great tension in the control room. When the program signed off, telephone switchboards at TV stations all over the nation lit up. It was the greatest reaction to a TV program up to that time.

Sprague Vonier, *Edward R. Murrow*. Milwaukee, Wisconsin: Gareth Stevens Children's Books, 1989.

In Milwaukee, Wisconsin, the state of McCarthy's birth, my parents sat in front of their tiny, fuzzy, television set in a flat on the west side and wept. "Maybe," my mother said, "it'll be over now."

Milwaukee, 1975

Last night when I called my brother to tell him about Christopher's death, I could feel his distress in the heavy silence that followed. Chris was in his twenties, about my brother's age, and his family and mine go back to the picket lines and union halls of the forties. In an unexpected way, the past had lunged into our present lives. My brother has his own apartment not far from where I live with two children in a community of women that includes my sister.

"Are you going to the funeral tomorrow?" I ask him. I already know my sister won't be there. She is still in some ways the baby sister.

"Should I?" Burr asked. "I mean, does it matter?

I wanted to say, *Come because it matters to me.* But I didn't, and then all day as I try to prepare myself for this funeral, memories come to me like dreams:

We are on our way to Milwaukee, sitting on the hard benches in the Arkansas airport. My mother, tired and rumpled, holds my baby sister on her lap. It is my job to watch Burr. He dashes away from me and then climbs up onto another bench to pull the hats off the heads of strange men, looking startled to be accosted by this little dark eyed boy.

The Milwaukee streets are grey and cold and foreign to us. The house on 34th Street where we temporarily stay with Walter's Aunt Adeline is dark and heavy with old furniture. Later, our parents inherited that huge house, built by a furrier at the turn of the century in what was once a grand neighborhood, one that is old now and deteriorating. These days our mother dotes on the stained glass windows, the marble fireplaces, the oak dining table where we now eat holiday dinners off the flowered china Aunt Adeline got at the Saturday matinees. But all that came later.

First, we live in a flat in an old duplex on Milwaukee's west side. We have little furniture but our beds. I spend most of my time shut inside my tiny bedroom reading. The babies have the run of our nearly empty flat..

At the end of my school day, Burr stands on the front stoop waving his skinny arms yelling, "Bug Tittie," meant to be Big Sister, humiliating me as I trudge up our street from the neighborhood public school I hate, the one where the kids pick on me for having curly hair and a southern accent, where the teachers treat all of us with cold, indifference.

I scream at my mother, "I can't bring anyone home from school!"

"Why not?" She doesn't get it.

"Because we have no furniture!" I scream at her, wanting her to feel bad.

She looks around the nearly empty living room. "You could always have a picnic on the floor," she says. I run into my bedroom and slam the door.

Later, walking slowly through the cemetery, I search the grounds for my brother. I feel as stiff inside as the sparse trees standing harshly against the winter sky. Then I see Burr in the distance, waiting with my mother. These days he stands over 6 feet tall, dark and long legged like me but thick in the arms and chest from years as a dock worker, years spent throwing bags of flour into the hold of some ship. He has his hands thrust into his pockets, his long, straight dark hair, so much like my mother's had been once, blowing across his face, his neck scrunched into his coat collar against the wind.

My mother is wearing her good black coat and is paying homage to this tragedy by dressing down-- gloves but only a small hat, no feathers. She has made up for all those years of poverty by becoming a fashion plate now that she's in her sixties. She says she believes people should go to demonstrations dressed as middle class citizens, so the "powers-that-be don't think it's only crazies demonstrating for justice." Our parents are active again--in their neighborhood organization, in the peace movement. I think about the anti-war demonstration of a few years ago when we all walked together downtown. My brother carried my baby son on his shoulders. It still makes me smile when I remember his tiny fist stuck up in the air above my brother's head.

Now, when I reach them, we stand in an awkward cluster making jokes about nothing, the family way of warding off pain. I glance over at the coffin and look quickly away. Then a voice rises above the wind telling us it is time to begin, and we move with the others forming a circle around the coffin. I hold back a little, staring down at the ground, trying to push back the horror of this death. His father begins to speak, and I feel my throat tighten against my tears. "In Christopher's memory," Nick says, "we must work even harder for peace and justice." I look up, and our eyes meet. His are heavy, the lids almost closed, but his brown eyes still sweet with love for all of us. Chris's mother, stands next to him, eyes closed, the grief etched into her face, and her body sways in the wind, light now, as if it's been emptied.

I remember Christopher saying to me years ago as we left a classroom together, "Your family and mine are lucky. We've avoided the bitterness of so many others like us because we had the love in our families to keep us strong."

"But Christopher," I answer him now, "it wasn't enough."

I feel my brother's hand take mine, pull me closer and squeeze. I look up, but his face is shielded by his collar. On the other side, my mother is crying. I close my eyes again and see myself a twelve year old, sitting on the floor, holding my little brother on my lap.

It is Christmas Eve in Milwaukee, 1953. My mother drags a scrawny tree in the door, dropping it on the living room floor, then dashing out to go find some presents. I try not to think about Grandpa's majestic tree of the year before. Walter and I get it standing up somehow. Then I make ornaments out of whatever I can find around the flat—ribbon, the funny papers, tin foil. The babies help: Burr dances around the tree; Lolly claps her hands in delight. I cook us food, something that isn't eggs or under done chicken. I lay it out on the table with paper towels folded into napkins under the cheap stainless. I am not yet twelve; it is my first dinner party.

Our mother comes back late, exhausted but triumphant. She has talked the store manager into helping her find presents she can afford for all of us. She is flushed with success. These days victories are rare. She notices the tree, the napkins, and the ornaments. I don't remember if she tells me that I've done a great, even heroic job. But I know it's one of the few happy memories I have of that flat.

Now, standing in the cemetery, my brother's hand in mine, I feel something let go inside. I am no longer listening to Nick, and I am crying for all of us, as much for the past as the present.

After the funeral, as we walk to a friend's house for lunch, Burr breaks the silence between us, "No one will ever understand what we went through," he says. I want to deny the words, but I can't. Somewhere inside they touch an old ache, the old loneliness. Once again, I am aware how much we have buried inside the family, how isolation became a way of life and how the secrets kept inside the family have bound us together and separated us from the rest of the world. There are parts of myself I never share outside this small circle. Once, it would have been dangerous, but now I have forgotten how.

Sitting with Burr on a small couch, a little apart from the others in the dusk that gathers around us, I begin to see how well we have hidden our pain even from each other. I have believed that my brother and sister, so much younger than I, were spared much of the misery of those years. His words uncoil slowly. "I must have felt their tension even in the womb." He pats his own stomach. "All that fear is still there. Your fears followed you to bed at night, surrounded you in dark places, but mine have just stayed trapped inside."

I see him dangling upside down from my mother's arms, his stomach distended, his tiny face red from crying. I see my baby sister in her sun bonnet on that Arkansas porch, and I remember how seldom she smiled that summer. Only a baby, I think now, and already she had learned to be sad. I lean over and touch Burr's arm because I am the one needing comfort, "There were good times, too," I say.

He smiles up at me. "Sure. We always laughed a lot. And I always respected the folks, even when I hated them for being different."

I can feel myself wanting to defend them like always, wanting to smooth everything out, like trying to smooth an unmade bed, hiding the lumpy sheets. "At least life was never dull," I say. "Think of all the good stories."

"The same ones over and over."

"Except Eve made women the heroes. For Grandpa, it was the working class, and Grandma, always gave God top billing. Remember how you and I gave all the stories numbers, and when one of them would start in, one of us would call out, "Number 34!""

"Melodramatic--all of them," he says, shaking his head in mock dismay, but there's a gleam in his eye.

I know if I push it, I can get him to begin laughing at their eccentricities. Suddenly, it seems terribly important not to laugh, not to give in to the impulse to make them into jokes. Once they had been our heroes; once we had suffered their losses over and over, reliving their migration from the farm to the labor movement, turning it into family myth, and still later, when the world began to cut them away like so much tree rot, we suffered with them in silence, keeping their secrets, always. "Burr," I say to my brother now, "with all the talk, all the stories, there is still a lot from those years we never talk about."

He looks up from his plate, the dark eyes wary now. He holds up his hand as if to shield himself against my words. "Look, digging around in this old stuff's not the answer. We cut our losses and go on. That's all."

"Sometimes, I feel like my life is still on hold."

"What are you waiting for?"

"I don't know. I want more than myths," I tell him.

"Myths aren't so bad," he says and smiles up at me ruefully. "Anyway, we cut our teeth on them."

"I want us to do more talking about those years we were followed from state to state and hunted down like criminals."

"Be careful," he says. "Taking out the past is like playing with a bomb, not knowing when it'll go off or who'll be hit."

For the first time, I find myself wondering if my mother is mostly silent about those years because she's afraid that the past could rise up and kill us. Does she think she's circumventing pain by silence? I see Christopher's eyes, the way they held mine in that classroom. "You mean, like what happened to Christopher."

"We don't know the past had anything to do with his death," my brother says, but his eyes don't quite meet mine.

We sit in silence. The air seems thicker, as if the colors of the past have bled into the room. Burr is looking down, leaning forward on his arms, opening and closing his fists like Grandpa used to do. But when he speaks again, his voice is just above a whisper. "Families don't always know," he says. He lifts his head and meets my gaze, and I am shocked to see tears in his eyes.

And then because I cannot yet sort it all out, but I want to share a little of these family secrets, and I want to give him comfort, I reach down into my memory and bring up this story, this piece of our early Milwaukee history. The bones of this incident I was told by my parents years ago, but I tell it now as a story that could be called: The End. It is the close of our family's six year struggle, and the beginning of the end of our own cold war:

Walter had been out in the truck all morning at his job delivering clean diapers and picking up the dirty ones. Somewhere on the outskirts of Milwaukee, almost at the end of his route, he began to sense something. He never allowed himself to completely relax, to stop waiting for the other FBI shoe to drop, so when he began to get that feeling that caused the hairs on the back of his neck to stand up, he looked into his rear view mirror. There was a dark sedan behind him that seemed to be coming along at a steady pace, one that stayed behind him through several turns. He sped up a bit and then some more until the curbs went whizzing by. He watched the sedan keep up with him. He could feel his stomach starting to rumble, his hands beginning to sweat on the steering wheel.

Suddenly, *without even knowing he had made a decision, he veered off the road and pulled over onto the shoulder. He looked in the side mirror and watched the sedan pull in back of the truck. He could see two men in the front seat, and he felt his face heat up. "Those assholes," he said out loud. Then he opened the truck door and jumped down. For a moment, he hesitated, seeing them still inside their car watching him through the windshield. He imagined they might even be smiling, looking forward to confronting him in person after all these years of phone calls, of whispers, of rumors. Then without fully knowing what he was about to do, he opened the back doors of the truck and turned his body toward them. His voice carried clearly through the morning air. "Want to see what I've got in here, what dangerous, subversive stuff I'm carrying?" Then he bent forward into the truck.*

The two men were getting out of the sedan. They wore grey raincoats, their hats tilted back on their heads. "We'd like talk to you..."one of them started to say. Then Walter emerged from inside the truck, his arms full of diapers, and before he could have said McCarthyism, he started flinging them at the men. "Here! Take these!" he yelled.

Diapers flew through the air. The men ducked. More diapers came at them, filling the sky like tiny sails, tossing and turning, then billowing to earth, covering the car, the ground, and as they fell, the air began to take on a sour smell that grew stronger, like a strange acid rain falling around them.

Now, the men covered their noses and grabbed for the door handles. One of them flung himself inside, while the driver paused outside the car. "Hey!" he called.

Walter had just emerged again from the truck, his hands full of soggy diapers. He hesitated at the sound of the man's voice, and for a long moment no one moved. Then Walter smiled and sent the next batch flying. The man ducked his head and raised a hand. Walter couldn't tell if it was to ward off the diapers, or a sign of surrender. But the car door slammed shut, and they took off backwards, spitting gravel into the air. He watched them until they pulled forward onto the road, passing the truck without even looking back. Then he took a deep breath and something lifted, an invisible shield, clear and hard as glass. He looked up at the sky half expecting to see fragments blowing free, and he saw, instead, that the grey had shifted into blue, and the sun had finally come out.

Walter twirled one last diaper, sending it sailing after them into the sky. For a moment he couldn't tell if he was laughing or crying. Then he said, "Got 'em the Christie way, killed 'em with germs." And he started to laugh. He stood there in the dust laughing, and then he picked up the diapers and drove home.

Epilogue: March, 2003

My cousin, Christie, and I get into our rental car and drive to Fort Smith Arkansas on a pilgrimage back to our grandparent's farm after nearly fifty years. The April sun beams down on us, and the temperature hovers around 70'. Christie has been here once, briefly. On the way, I remind her of the year I spent here. But I don't speak of the dread I have been holding in for days. "It will be an adventure," everyone says. But they don't know about the shame I have buried about being the daughter of a "red" or the pain of separation from friends made and lost.

Pulling into Fort Smith, it is oddly comforting to see the familiar look of suburban sprawl. I spot a Starbucks, TGIF Friday, places I spurn when I am home in Milwaukee, Wisconsin, preferring local businesses over chains. But here where I have expected-what? A posse to ride out and lasso us? The Ku Klux Klan to greet us? Here, I feel relief at the dull familiarity of a Starbucks logo. And when we get out of the car, the southern breeze, soft against my face, lifts my spirits a bit.

Our suite is comfortable and quiet and everyone from housekeeping to desk clerks are so nice that I find myself smiling more than I have in public places for a long time. Instead of being run out of town on a rail, it seems we are being welcomed everywhere with that famous southern hospitality I had forgotten. Friendliness softens back muscles.

That night, I find that I am able to sleep, a deep dreamless sleep.

The next day, Monday, it is even warmer, and we happily kill time. I am startled by a huge billboard advertising their phone book and proclaiming in oversized red letters: *Think Red.* I burst out laughing, saying to Christie, "You'd never have seen *that* in 1953!" Back then it had been "dangerous red," "dirty red," "the red menace."

At a local restaurant, we eat fried catfish, fried okra, and three kinds of shrimp, and greens and sweet potato fries with sweet buttery syrup to dip them in and hush puppies and corn casserole. I am in heaven. For dessert, we indulge in blackberry cobbler, and when the sweet biscuit dough melts into my mouth, the Mansfield grade school cafeteria floats across my mind, and I feel the warmth of those lady cooks who had once over-fed a skinny northern kid, hungry for their food.

On Monday, it has cooled back down to 65' but still feels like a heat wave to my northern blood. We head toward the county seat of Greenwood to get a map and directions out to our eighty acres of neglected land. We are told which streets to take out of town and to dive along Top Fork Road until we recognize our land. Our eyes meet. We are thinking the same thing: will we recognize this land?

At first the houses are fairly close together. Nothing looks familiar. They're almost all newer houses, ranch style. But then suddenly, the houses stop and on both sides of the road it is brambles and brush. "Is this it?" Christie wants to know. But

I can't be sure with nothing to mark it but these strange twisted trees. We drive on and soon, we come to the place where the hill drops down. Suddenly, I am there, on my bike and riding as fast as I can down this hill to Brenda's house. "It's the right hill," I tell Christie, hearing the excitement in my voice. "And over on the right, should be the Whittaker house." As soon as the words are out of my mouth, we pass a broken down house, its boards bleached grey-white by the sun but no cherry trees. "There should be cherry trees," I tell her. And then we see one, a small one, a stringer tree, all by itself on the side just like I knew it should be. Then we are starting down the hill and at the bottom, where the land has been cleared for pasture, I slow down to read the name on the mailbox. There it is: Whittaker.

When we get back up to the top of the hill and come around the curve, this time I know it's the right curve. It's like the hill. My body feels it. We pull over onto the strip of mowed grass by the edge of the road, and I get out, walk a few feet and turn toward the road.

"What's different about this curve?" Christie asks. A fair question. But I know because I have stood on this spot a hundred times, waiting for a car we can hear but can't yet see to come around that bend and break the boredom of the day. If I close my eyes, I can hear my grandmother at the screen door, her voice happy as she says, "Why it's the Owen's. Hope they've time for a visit." In a minute, Brenda

Owens will jump down from the back of their pick-up.

I take a breath. The road is empty. I haven't felt stillness like this in a long time, so thick around me it's hard to imagine any sound can ever break through. As an eleven year old, I longed for noise. Now, I stand here and let the silence cover me like an old, familiar orlon blanket.

Christie comes to stand next to me, and we turn to stare a moment into the brush. But we're not ready for that, not yet. We go back to the car and drive slowly toward town. As we round the corner, a golf cart covered in heavy plastic comes into sight. We can see a man, a woman and a child sitting snugly inside. I slow down and stop. The man reaches into a mailbox, but they are watching us as well. I roll down the window and call out. "Hi, that's quite a contraption you have there." Then I see the name on his mailbox, and something clicks in my memory. A grey haired man pushes out of the plastic. I smile. "I'm Christine," I say, "and my grandparents used to live just down the road."

"The Christie place." He says it as a statement. He moves toward our car as he says, "We went to school together." He leans in the window. "I've wondered what happened to *you?*" My heart skips a beat. Does he mean he wondered about *me,* or does he really mean he's wondered about *us,* about that notorious family that got run out of town? I want to ask him, but the words clog in my throat from years of holding them back. Instead, I ask if he remembers Edna Dale. In my mind's eye, I see her standing next to my mother in her white graduation dress, her skin all peaches and cream. "Died of cancer last year," he says sadly.

"That's a shame, "I say and think: *So much for envy.* "And Paula?" I ask.

"She's a VP at the Mansfield Bank," he says

We chat a bit more. He says our old school is still there, and I say I don't know if I'd even recognize my old house in town. He says to drive down the main street and I'll know my house when I see it.

Then we're on our way again. In a few minutes, we are in Mansfield and turning left at the Tasty Freeze like he told us and going straight out Main Street. Once again, the houses are new, and I'm not recognizing a thing until I see the creek, the one where the water moccasins played and worried my mother. Once again, it is the land that speaks to me and not the buildings or the people. The house we pass has been newly painted, blue, while ours had been white, but then I notice that the pillars are still white. "There it is," I tell my cousin, and we slow down and stare out of the window.

A man pulls into the driveway, gets out, sees us, nods and goes into the house. I almost call out to him, but then I think, why? What do I have to tell him? What does it matter to him that I lived here for one year a long time ago, that I had flowers on the wall paper in my bedroom, that my mother once killed a mouse in the kitchen with a straw broom, that she painted her bedroom red. No one remembers my grandmother's banana cream cake or the eight foot Christmas tree Grandpa tied to the living room ceiling. They don't care how happy my mother was to leave or how much I cried.

But the next day, we drive back out to the Christie land, pull over again into the mowed area and get out of the car, determined to take on the brush. "Where do you think the house used to be?" my cousin wonders. But I know because I know the curve, and I walk a few feet into the brambles, stop and face out to the road. I know we won't find much because after old age finally forced our grandparents out, the sheriff burned the house some years later to keep out squatters. But there must be something left. I am wondering if I should get my boots out of the car or just push on in with my tennis shoes. I take a few tentative steps into the brush, but the brambles push me back.

Gradually, I find a few openings, and then suddenly almost stumble over a large chunk of concrete that might be part of a chimney. Christie has followed me, more tentative about taking on this wild land, but then we both see the refrigerator door, lying, partially covered by brambles, brown with rust. And then a few feet later, a set of rusted bed springs. We laugh, delighted by these finds, these crusty relics. For me, the land is saying: someone slept here on those sweltering summer nights when you lay on your cot, listening to the drone of insects mingle with their snores, hearing your own heartbeat. You did live here. And I breathe in the smells that are amazingly familiar: Arkansas pine smell mixed with the charred wood of a stove banked for the day. The scent of strawberries drifts in the air, although there are none here, at least not that I can see. But once, grandma, her cheeks red from the heat, had put them on the wooden kitchen table in an old crockery bowl, red and juicy every morning for breakfast. It all happened--the loneliness, the love, the pain--all of it. This land has been here all along waiting for one of us to come back.

We left all those places of my childhood and never looked back. And even when in later years, I tried to find those houses again, they had fallen to progress or decay, and it was hard to tell if they had ever been there: the apartment building in Chicago torn down to make a playground, the yellow house in California long gone to urban blight, the tar paper house in Denver so erased that when my cousins and I tried to find it in 2000, we couldn't even be sure we had the right street. Whenever I visited those places, I had been living in the family pain. For the first time, I realize how we have dragged the trauma of those years with us everywhere we went and then finally, to Milwaukee.

Our parents struggled through those early years in Milwaukee, working at any job they could get, and eventually built a new life. Evelyn went back to college in her 50's, earning a B.S. degree and going on to work in community mental health. Walter worked for the State of Wisconsin. They lived their belief in racial integration by staying in their west side neighborhood after people of color began moving in, refusing to participate in white flight and actively working against red lining by real estate companies. They walked in open housing marches with Father Groppi in the 1960's, worked in freedom schools, demonstrated against the war in Vietnam long before their children did. They never gave up the struggle, and they continued to work for peace and justice.

As for their children: my sister, the baby who rarely smiled, perhaps bore the most obvious wounds. She lived quietly and died of an aneurysm in 2000, much loved by family and friends for her toughness and her kindness. My brother, the adored toddler, helped establish an underground high school newspaper in the 1960's, participated in his generation's anti-war movement and worked on the Milwaukee docks. These days he invests his energy in alternative health care with a thriving business in Milwaukee as a cranial/sacral therapist.

I spent time in the 1960's and 1970's in Milwaukee's Community Schools, administered an alternative school and helped to organize and run a free health clinic. I returned to school earning an M.F.A. in English and for seventeen years taught courses in writing and Ethnic Studies at a state university.

We are fairly typical of this group of red diaper babies who have so often grown up to work for progressive causes. We are journalists, health care workers, musicians, educators. We continue to work for change both globally and locally all across this country. But you may never know that we come from families that bore the brunt of this country's cold war hysteria. Most of us carry our wounds in secret places, seldom revealed to anyone outside our small circles. And often, we have hidden these wounds even from each other. "Sometimes," I once told a friend whose family had also suffered during the 1950's, "I feel like an abused child."

He took a deep breath, and then he said, "Now, that we've made our peace with America, maybe the true battle will be trying to forgive each other."

Today, as I bend and push my way through the bramble, moving slowly, cautiously, breaking twigs, stepping over piles of brush, I see signs that others have intruded, have borrowed this space for a time-- bottles lie in the weeds, beer cans, their labels still readable; there are signs of banked campfires. I turn and see that the road has disappeared. I am completely hidden here, surrounded by these grey-black trees, their branches gnarled and twisted by dry rot, they bend inward, and their roots tangle together in the brush; they are what remain of our grandfather's monumental effort to wrest pasture from this wild landscape.

I almost retreat. But curiosity is stronger than fear. Instead, I bend branches in front of me and press on. Space clears, the forest opens before me. It is not impenetrable after all. A bird calls somewhere near, and I look toward the sky and watch as it swoops above me and then soars overhead, toward tall trees I can now glimpse in the distance. They, too, have been here all along. I stop and breathe in the warm earth. My grandfather's voice rises from memory: "There are only two things worth dying for: land and justice." Towering to the west, the tall pines, his pines, have been quietly growing in the back of this land for fifty years. They grow straight, their bark still firm, their tops reach into the sunlight. They, too, have been waiting, standing proud on the Christie land. The briar will not claim them; they have refused to lie down and die. Today, standing here in the sunshine, surrounded by brambles, I feel ready to keep working to find that forgiveness. It has taken me a long time to see our parents as flawed but remarkably courageous human beings, American heroes largely unsung by history books. I hope that I am singing them at last.

Acknowledgements:

My undying gratitude for the many friends who read bits and pieces of this book along the way and gave encouragement when my spirits flagged and to Ian Harris who first said to me that this story should be in print and to Tom Schwarz who kept my computer running against all odds and most especially, to Tom Moylan who read the shaky beginnings of it all and never stopped encouraging me to keep writing it. And to Roger Bybee who told me to be bold like my mother. It takes a village to produce a book.

Thanks to the University of North Carolina-Greensboro MFA in writing program for giving me two important years to write, and to think of myself as a writer. In particular, love to Fred Chappell, one of this country's finest writers, who took the time to make comments on an earlier draft.

Love and thanks to the Milwaukee Writers Group: Bill Murtaugh, Jane Thompson, Jon Kolb and Sprague Vonier who patiently listened and commented through many excerpts of this memoir over nearly twenty years.

And also to the Tuesdays: My "new" writers group in Oregon who welcomed me to the group, listened with open minds and hearts and gave me the acceptance I badly needed to finish. And especially to Linnea Harper who generously copy edited.

Much love to my family who share this history and especially my children, Sam and Robin who often gave up time and attention during the early years of writing.

Special love and gratitude to my oldest granddaughter, Caitlin Christie Bergeon, who designed the cover for this book and whose wit and friendship have nourished me in my dotage.

And my deepest gratitude goes to my daughter, Robin Christie Raber, a talented poet herself, who generously gave her time to read and to listen while I talked my way through many drafts and struggled to bring this into being. In particular, a trip back from Madison when I read out loud while she drove, and we both cried all the way home. Without her deep listening and thinking, this book would never have happened.

References

Caute, David. *The Great Fear. The Anti Communist Purge Under Truman and Eisenhower.* New York: Simon and Schuster, 1978.

Hellman, Lillian. Introduction. *The Big Knockover.* By Dashiell Hammett. Ed. Lillian Hellman. New York: Vintage Books, 1972. v-xxv.

Kahn, Albert E. *High Treason: The Plot Against the People.* New York: Lear Pub., 1950.

Morgan, Ted. *Reds: McCarthyism in Twentieth Century America.* New York: Random House, 2003.

Navasky, Victor. *Naming Names.* New York: Penguin Books, 1981.

Vonier, Sprague. *Edward R. Murrow.* Milwaukee: Gareth Stevens Children's Books, 1989.

Wills, Gary. Introduction. *Scoundrel Time.* By Lillian Hellman. Boston: Little, Brown and Company, 1976. 3-34.

Zinn, Howard. *A People's History of the United States.* New York: Harper Colophon Books, 1980.

CPSIA information can be obtained at www.ICGtesting.com
Printed in the USA
BVOW031246051011

272874BV00001B/35/P